Getaway.

Even more *funny signs*

Hilarious messages from Africa and beyond

RS&P 75 *Great years*

Ramsay, Son & Parker
Cape Town, South Africa

Every month for nearly two decades we've been chuckling at pictures of signs our well-travelled readers send in. About 10 years ago, it occurred to us to put them into a book. In that first edition, the then editor-in-chief, David Steele, wrote that 'while some of the signs might amuse us in the naivety or ignorance of English grammar, let no-one say we are mocking those who made them. On the contrary, we salute their ingenuity, skill and spirit.'

The first book hit the presses as *Funny Signs*, although at the time we had no idea it would be so enthusiastically received, going into five reprints. It also produced a flurry of ever more funny signs which, in 2004, led to another book, *More Funny Signs*.

Writing in that edition, then *Getaway* editor David Bristow called it 'a tribute to the readers of *Getaway*, who share with us and all other readers the spirit of their journeys through these hilarious, poignant, silly, ridiculous and often bewildering signs.'

The first edition co-incided with our magazine's 10th anniversary, the second with its 15th. We could hardly fail to put out another edition on our 20th: *Even More Funny Signs*. All that time, the signs have been rolling in. It's amazing how many people go to considerable trouble to tell other people wacky things on boards – and often get the message so delightfully wrong doing it.

Something that has changed since our first edition is that South Africans, from whom most of the signs come, have greatly expanded their travel destinations, particularly to the East. It is from there, in what has come to be known as Chinglish (Chinese English) that some of the real corkers are found. We at *Getaway* are sure you'll enjoy our third journey into public oddity.

Don Pinnock

This book is dedicated to all *Getaway's* readers, who span the globe.

Getaway

Publisher: Jacqueline Lahoud

Edited by: Don Pinnock

Compiled by: Khumo Ntoane

Sub-editor: Marion Whitehead

Art Director: Rob House

Designer: Megan Knox

Printed and bound by: Imago in Malaysia
Job No. 000803

First published by Jacana Media (Pty) Ltd,
in association with *Getaway* Magazine, 2008
10 Orange Street, Sunnyside,
Auckland Park 2092,
South Africa
+27-11-628-3200
www.jacana.co.za

ISBN 978-1-77009-520-5

Chapters

Children: I came across this sign in the heart of Uganda, close to the Equator and a few kilometres from the River Nile. Brian Wilkins.

Shopping the African way

Does that apply to the Coke, the building or the goods inside? Karen van der Westhuizen of Cape Town found this little shop on a lonely road in Namibia.

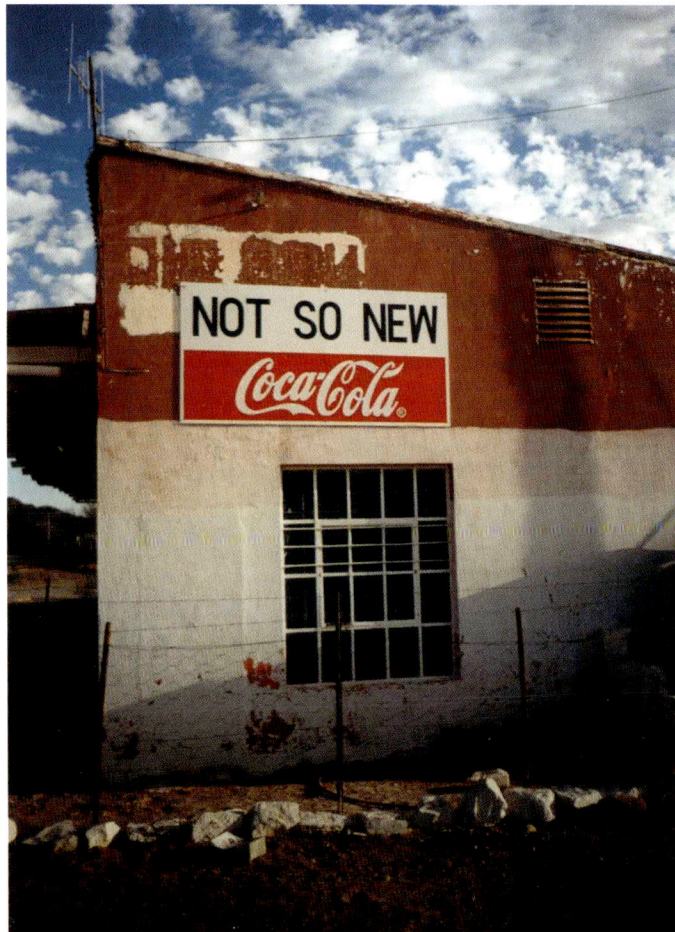

Kuntz Coetzee would love to know what's in the ketchup in Francistown.

Subtlety wasn't a norm in the old days. Carla van der Sandt of Durban found a sign made in the 1800s in Hoedspruit.

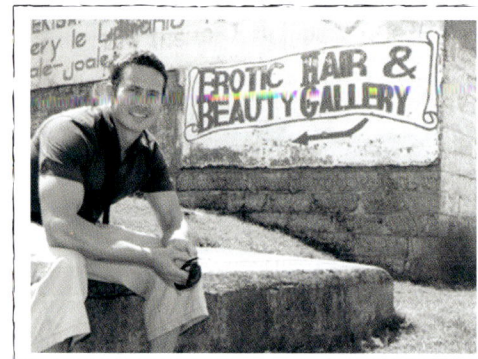

Maybe someone's English was a bit shaky. On the other hand, perhaps they really mean it. This was taken in Morija, Lesotho, by Riaan de Kock of Stellenbosch.

BELOW: It seems that although the cost of living might be on the rise, death comes cheap, as this sign spotted in Klerksdorp by Ohna Norval of Weltevreden Park shows.

ABOVE: Heindrich Eksteen of Windhoek wasn't quite sure about the placement of the full stop and we weren't sure about the quality of the goods inside. But it was near Duiwelskloof so anything's possible.

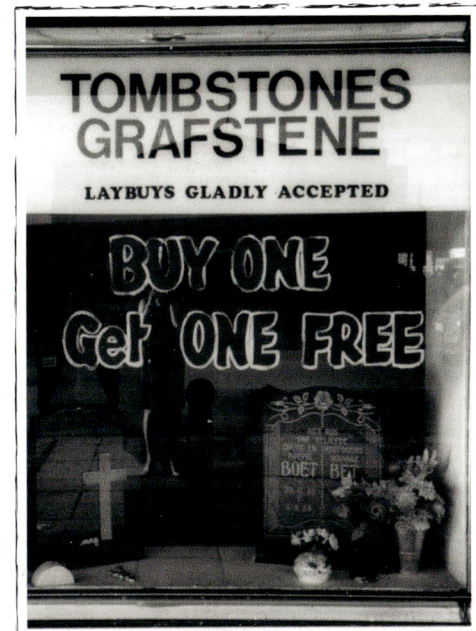

The Cintsa minimart is a one-stop shop for Coke, sperm, you name it. Steve Jiraz of George spotted this sign while holidaying in the Eastern Cape. Wonder if he offered his services?

Get all your soul and shoe repairs done here. Taken in KwaNokuthula just outside Plettenberg Bay by David Ritchie.

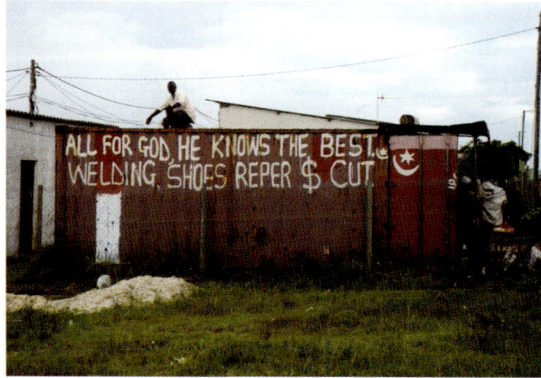

Obviously at some shops you can get yourself branded for a pittance. Malcolm Hickman in Mayville.

Chris Jacobs saw this sign in Vryburg. Makes you wonder what bits of themselves people hand over as scrap.

It's so honest it's scary! This photo was taken outside Mokopane on the Marken Road turnoff by Charlene Smit.

BELOW: How many sheets do you use to use them slightly? Bernd Ader.

RIGHT: Is fish the new meat? Anabela Peixoto of Joburg found a butchery in St Lucia that seemed to think so.

Margaret Rushton of Broederstroom wondered if they lasted a lifetime.

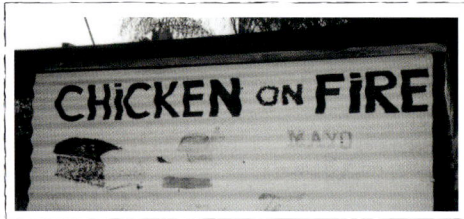

Hopefully someone put it out. Sent by Sarah Venter.

CHICKEN ON FIRE

coca cola
GOD KNOWS
TUCK SHOP

Seems flies in Zambia are averse to the cold. David Malan, Pretoria.

Well, we thought it would be only God who would know where it is (between nowhere and nothing). Fredre and Loudene Heunis, Gauteng.

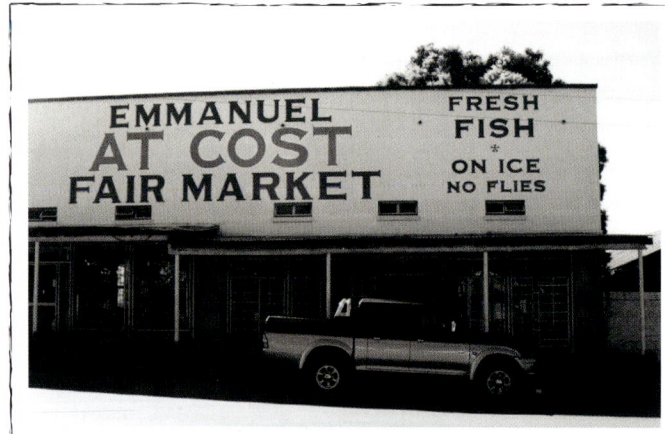

Talk about bush meat! Needless to say, John and Kathy Nightingale didn't risk it.

LAPRIMA THE BEST QUALITY FOOD & SNAKES

EXPERIENCE THE BEST QUALITY FOOD WITH EXCELLENT SERVICE

Johann and Jovita Stander of Centurion wondered whether you chopped your grocer into your chicken or cooked them separately.

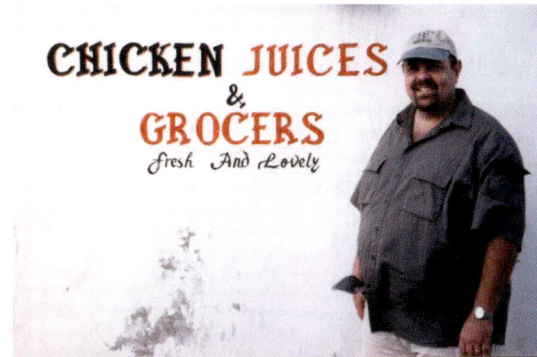

CHICKEN JUICES & GROCERS
fresh And Lovely

RIGHT: Looks like biltong, tastes like chicken, might just be human. Taken outside a garage in Ellisras. Pinette Atkinson, Botswana.

Coca-Cola

HUMAN BILTONG KIOSK
TEL: 014 763 5101
BOEREWORS
MAALVLEIS
BILTONG
CHILLIBITES
HOENDERVLEIS

Nando's advertising has always been smart, but this is pushing it, especially when you are just outside Kruger Park. Antonie Jordaan, Hoedspruit.

Charmaine Smit discovered that not only was Ronnie's Sex Shop famous, but it's extended its business! This picture was taken on Route 62 near Calitzdorp.

ATTENTION
Clients are not allowed to:
- Sit on the balcony.
- Dress or undress in the restaurant.
- Put your baby on the table.

Free massage by woodpecker included, though it could hurt a bit. Tim Hrusa from Gaborone saw this one in the village of Metsimotlhabe on the way to Khutse Game reserve, Botswana.

That's what you get when you open a restaurant between a strip club and a preschool. Noticed in La Digue by Doris Schulz, Seychelles.

BACKPECKERS
BED & BREAKFAST
OVERNIGHT ACCOMMODATION
TEL: 74344493
→

NOTICE-PUBLIC BAR
OUR PUBLIC BAR IS PRESENTLY NOT OPEN BECAUSE IT IS CLOSED. MANAGER

Yebo! Taken in Mozambique by Sarah Pennington.

Obviously nobody harries you at this watering hole. Found by Kurt Woerzer, Dalton.

We skipped lunch. Steve and Rene Watson saw this sign in Vilanculos, Mozambique.

BELOW: Yebo! Taken in Mozambique by Sarah Pennington.

This is along the road between Lebowakgomo and Jane Furse in Limpopo. Brian Jones, North West.

Taken somewhere between Gaberone and Khutse Reserve in Botswana. I have heard of a person throwing his name away in a bar, but the bar itself losing its name? Mike Brink.

An odd sign in Pilgrim's Rest. We wondered what was for lunch. Hugh and Sandra Verreynne.

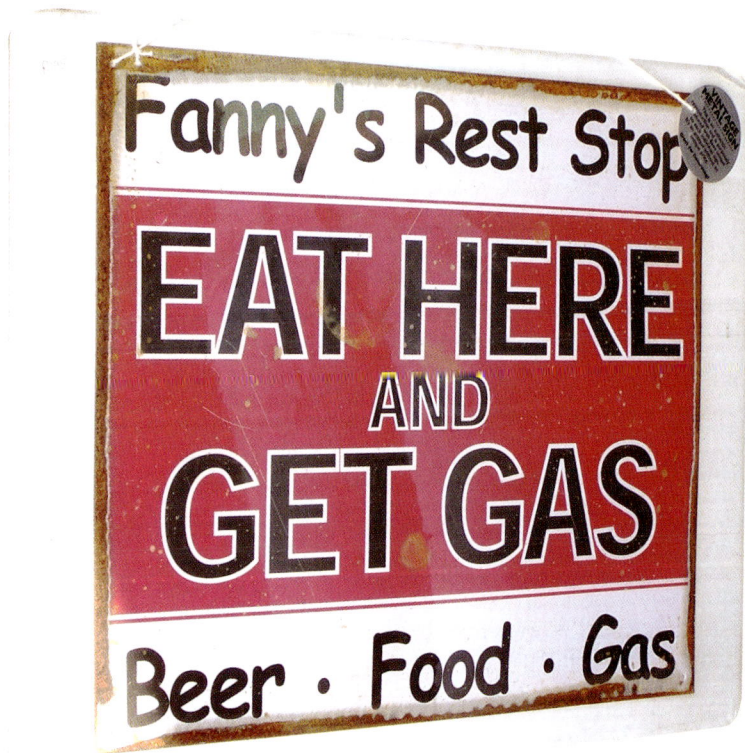

Fanny's Rest Stop
EAT HERE AND GET GAS
Beer · Food · Gas

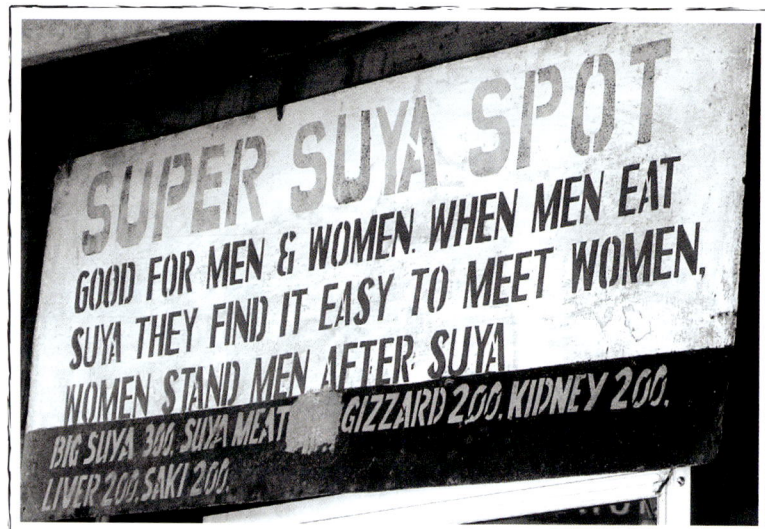

SUPER SUYA SPOT
GOOD FOR MEN & WOMEN. WHEN MEN EAT SUYA THEY FIND IT EASY TO MEET WOMEN, WOMEN STAND MEN AFTER SUYA
BIG SUYA 300. SUYA MEAT ... GIZZARD 200. KIDNEY 200. LIVER 200. SAKI 200.

Wow! Just what is this stuff? Taken in Nigeria by Peter Dacre.

Bruce Jenkins of Pietermaritzberg says he finally found the G-spot.

For sporty types or people with chicken pox? Ray Airosa came across this place in Oshikango, Namibia.

Donkey meat? Taken en route from Johannesburg to Madikwe Game Lodge, Northern Province. From Angela and Gordon.

Gerald and Sue McCay of Umtentweni, found out the secret ingredient to good quality boerewors. Whether you eat boerewors again is up to you.

Looking for quality meat? Try Jeffery's But. Spotted by Heather Murton.

This is the name of a shop in Nata, Botswana. We weren't sure if you could buy only wild beasts here or if you could get other meats as well. Norma Leviton.

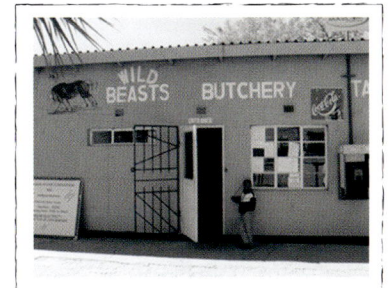

Andre Vermaak of Braken Gardens found this chilly message in Euro-Disney.

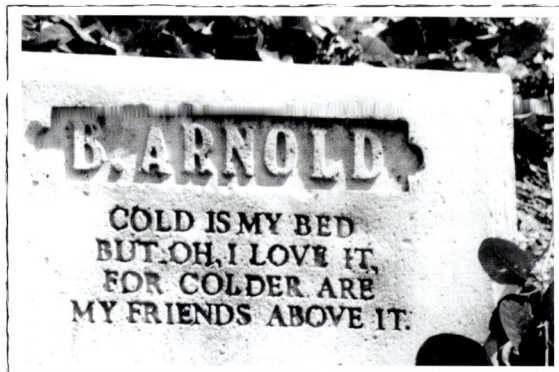

B. ARNOLD

COLD IS MY BED
BUT, OH, I LOVE IT,
FOR COLDER ARE
MY FRIENDS ABOVE IT.

FELICITY CORPSE DECORATION

0243186796
0242949843

Location. AFRIKIKO
KOFFE KROM
OBUASI

The last makeover, Ghana. Eva Noble.

You've heard of the film *Four Weddings and a Funeral*? Snapped in Vryburg by Keith Robinson.

This funeral home will B there 4 U. Seen in Qwa Qwa by Brenda Garth-Davis.

Anyone in this queue in the Tsitsikamma area could end up with a very long wait.
Sent by Mel Hancke, Cape Town.

W McLeary of Helderberg was surprised to find that your luck may not run out completely when you die....

Joelene du Toit of Môreskof enjoyed the ambiguity of Thothela's Funeral Parlour in Koster.

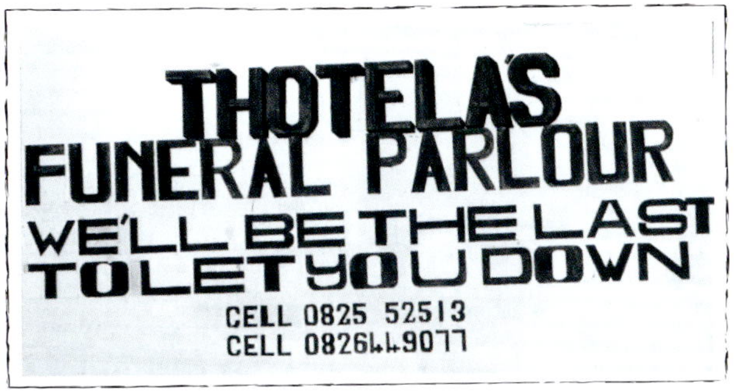
THOTELA'S
FUNERAL PARLOUR
WE'LL BE THE LAST
TO LET YOU DOWN
CELL 0825 52513
CELL 0826449077

Photographed at the Langebaan Farmhouse Hotel. Simon Perkin.

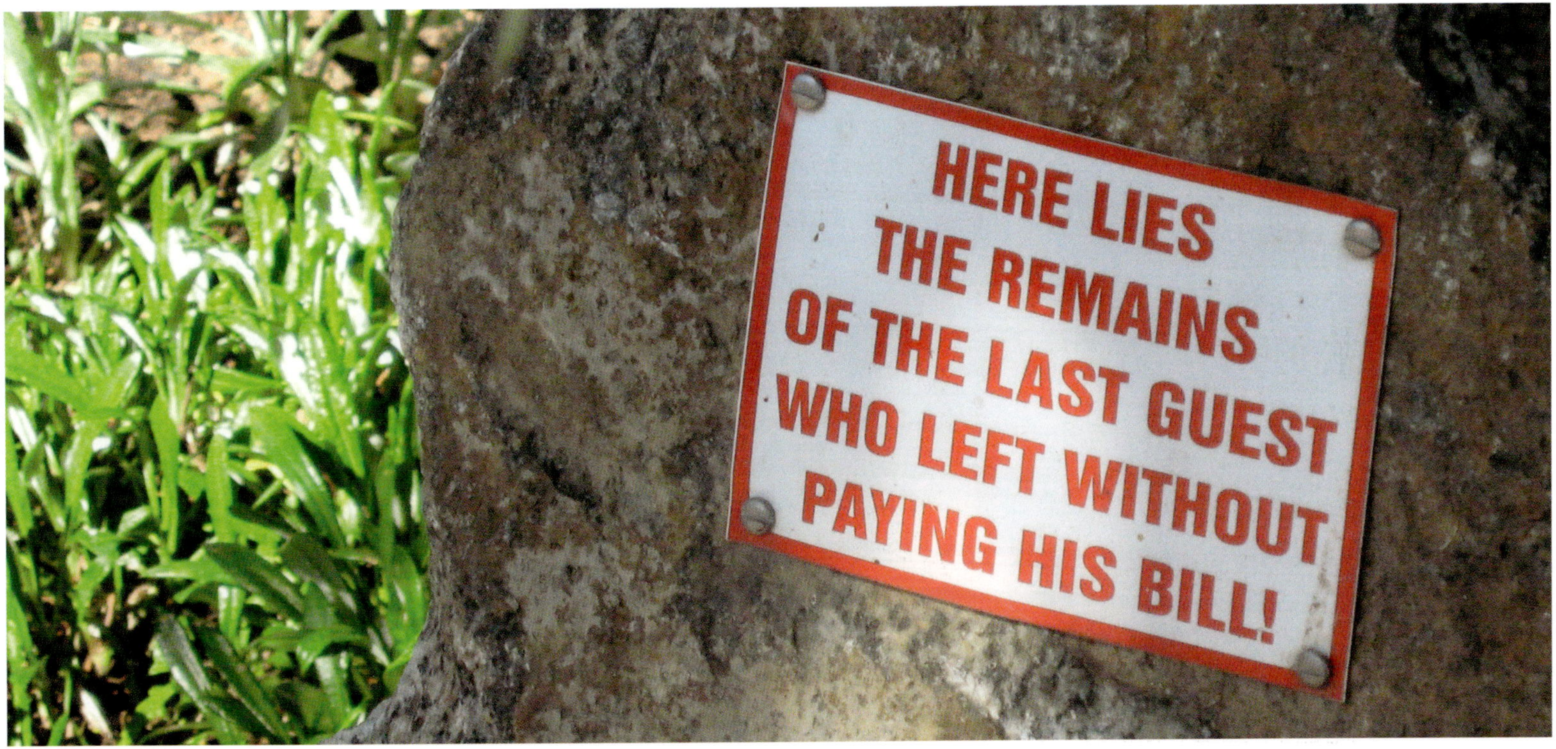
HERE LIES
THE REMAINS
OF THE LAST GUEST
WHO LEFT WITHOUT
PAYING HIS BILL!

We are expats living in Zambia. Good thing we have excellent clinics as well. Heike and Uwe Niederheitmann, Zambia.

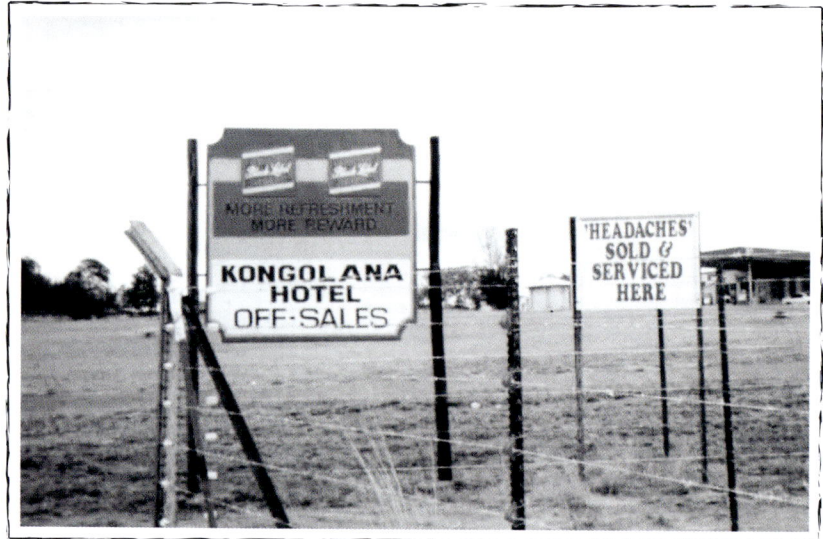

There are many ways to describe a hangover. Here's where you can get yours polished and buffed up. Spotted by John Crowson, Underberg.

Every hangover dream is to find one of those babbalaas clinics. Maria Nel found a sign for one in Mozambique.

DR. ISAC
HEALING GENERAL
ASTHMA & TB   LOST LOVER
ARBOTION   ENLARGEMENT
STUDY PROBLEM
MAN & WOMEN PROBLEM
CELL:0794500652 →

I wonder if medical aid will cover the cost of my lost lover? Spotted in Belfast, Mpumalanga by Ritha De Lange.

Sure we'll keep our *seevoëls* and dassies leashed and away from the restaurant. As for the stray animals, let's hope they can read. The owner of this sign spotted by Graham and Sheila Morris oustide Club Mykonos, Langebaan, doesn't sound like someone we'd leave our pets with when we go on holiday.

**VOETSEK
@#$%&*
SEEVOËLS, HONDE, DASSIES & KATTE**

**PLEASE BE PATIENT
AVERAGE WAITING
TIME 30 MIN**

NOTICE
NO INDIGENOUS
TREES OR
VEGETATION
TO BE USED
FOR FIRES.
PLEASE USE BINS

Better plumbing might help reduce the waiting time. The kids seemed pretty patient, though. This sign was sent in by Michelle Lumlry of Mooi River.

Wonder how often they have to replace burned bins? Found by Karl-Louis van Heerden In Igoda Mouth, East London.

I'm not sure how you would get this right, but we drove safely just in case. Norma Leviton.

DON'T KICK YOURSELF BLIND! ROAD SAFETY BEGINS WITH YOU.

RIGHT: In Malawi, that's very true. Lauren Hesom.

BELOW: After driving a long detour, it was good of them to warn us of the consequences to our health. Xen Ludick, Johannesburg.

POLICE SLOW

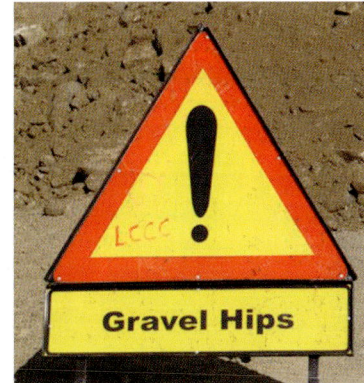

LCCC
Gravel Hips

Sigh! They always did get picked on. Nic Spring saw this sign in a restaurant window in Kalk Bay, Cape Town.

You can say that again! This was on a sand road near Oranjemund, Namibia. Pierre Nel, Boksburg.

There seem to be some people who think they have special privileges. Marion Baird took this photo on a road through a vineyard outside Plettenberg Bay.

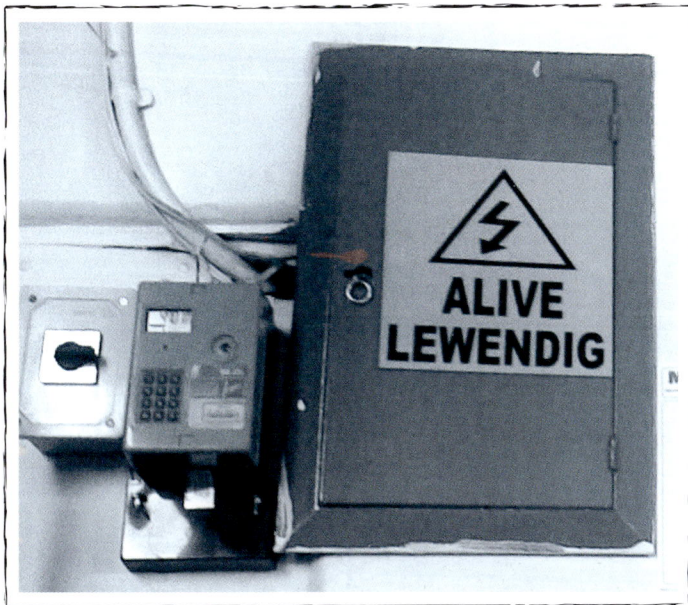

Obviously someone's attempt at reviving Frankenstein. Seen in Middelburg, Mpumalanga, at a business premises by Gert Beetge of Middelburg.

I spotted this sign at the Keurbooms River close to Plettenberg Bay. I would never have called water slippery. Karel du Toit.

PASOP
GLADDE OPPERVLAKTE

BEWARE
SLIPPERY SURFACE

Drunken people crossing

This sign was at a major intersection between two clubs at Patong Beach in Phuket. Sent by Wayne Monk.

At that pace even the snails will get there before you. Sent by Tracey Shaw

Strickly 10 km/h

Shirylee Wyngaard found this sign in Victoria Falls Airport in Zimbabwe – maybe ET the alien was forgetting to call home.

IS THERE LIFE AFTER DEATH?

TRESPASS HERE AND FIND OUT

No need to say more. Susan Beukes found this sign on a hiking trail in Knysna.

Would this be no entry for cars or boats? Sent in by Eddie Hawkey and taken in Kruger National Park.

Wonder what cheese has to do with speed limits? Sent by Derek Beatty.

Clearly one of the more severe hazards of being in a wheelchair. Taken at St Lucia Crocodile Centre by Menoli Gounden of Durban.

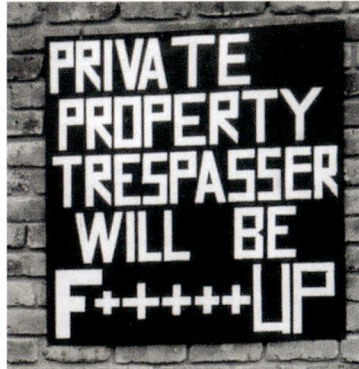

Don't say you haven't been warned. Thinus Malherbe sent this sign taken in Limpopo.

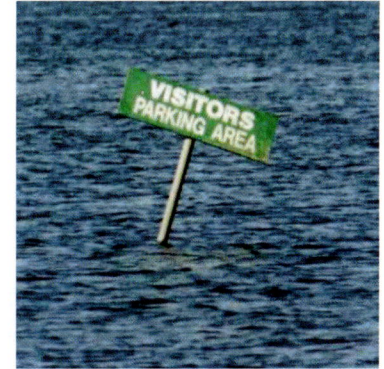

In Namibia they seem to have an easy way of getting rid of irritating tourists. The reason, though, was the heavy rains near Henties Bay, where Bernd Meyer spotted this sign.

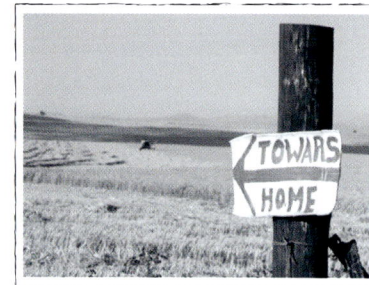

You won't get lost, will you? Louise Smit sent us this sign from Misverstand Dam, Western Cape.

I drove past, had to reverse and take this picture as it made total sense. I was on my way to Lake Naivasha in Kenya, close to Nairobi. Kobus Portwig.

Not sure where this is but, if you get there, you've been warned. Jan Zieda, Vanderbijlpark.

Where is the parking then? Willy and Margaret von Lochem found this sign in a French ski resort.

WELCOME IN VAL THORENS
CAR PARK FORBIDEN
IN THE RESORT
COMPULSORY PARKING

Where to next? Peter Strosbacs was confused when he reached this sign on the road to the Hoba meteorite near Grootfontein, Namibia.

N'OUBLIEZ PAS DE RENDRE VOTRE CLEF AVANT DE QUITTER L'HOTEL.
MERCI ET BONNE ROUTE.

DON'T FORGETGIVE YOURS KEYS BEHIND TO START THE HOTEL
THANK YOU AND GOOD TRAVEL

I think I'll be stick to my terrible French. Chris Waddel.

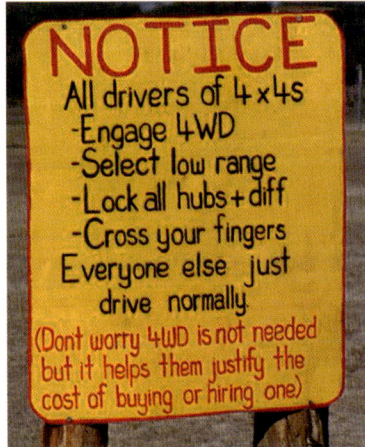

NOTICE

All drivers of 4×4s
- Engage 4WD
- Select low range
- Lock all hubs + diff
- Cross your fingers

Everyone else just drive normally.

(Don't worry 4WD is not needed but it helps them justify the cost of buying or hiring one)

This one speaks for itself! Susan Venter, Tzaneen, found this sign in Ngepi Nature Reserve.

Maybe Syria has secret short cuts. Andre Bossenkol and his wife (pictured) found the sign on their way from Amsterdam (Netherlands) to Stellenbosch. The co-ordinates are N34.70537 E36.30056.

Does it slip all the way to the pool? Pippa Prior, Johannesburg.

CAUTION POO SLIPPERY

C Scholtz, Somerset West, urges all drivers to fill up before reaching Maun, as the petrol station doesn't offer any for sale.

You have been warned! Taken by Kathleen Kamstra along the Cathcart-Hogsback Road, Eastern Cape.

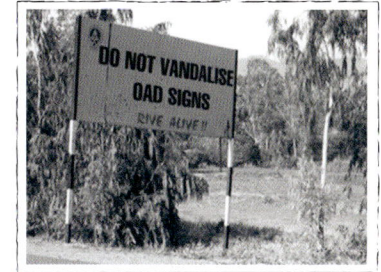

We came across this sign in Phwezi, Northern Malawi. Josh Mostert, Harare.

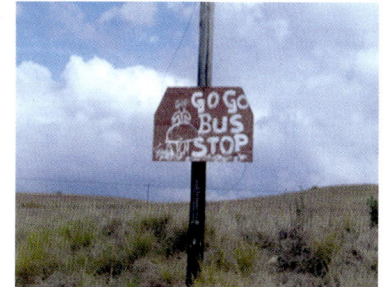

Only slow coaches are permitted to stop here for the *gogos* (grannies). Taken near Kestel in the Eastern Free State. Gillian Gotte.

U-turns seen from a different angle, by Chris Sherwood.

LEFT: They grow them big near Brits, though Emmarentia Kloppers of Boksburg was a bit nervous to investigate the giant frogs this sign promised.

Makes one wonder whether you're coming or going! Nigel Fuller snapped these odd markings in Ramsgate, KwaZulu-Natal.

There are bad roads, there are awful roads and then there are those that provoke irate graffiti. This was taken by Frans Coetsee on a 'kak pad' near Lambert's Bay in the Western Cape.

Trudi Roussouw found a sign that helped her a lot with water restrictions.

STOP
4
BESPAAR WATER
DRINK WYN
CONSERVE WATER

KAK Pad

R355 Lambertsbaai →
Palesheuwel
R365
Piketberg

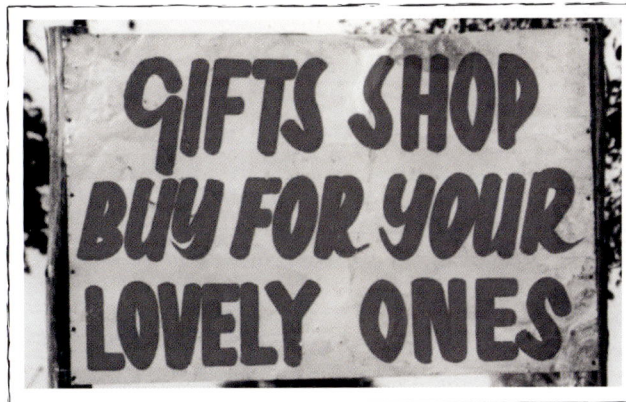

GIFTS SHOP
BUY FOR YOUR
LOVELY ONES

ABOVE: Jailes Andesme Jacobs of Tygervalley who sent in this sign says he thought it was a '*bak*' pad rather than a '*kak pad*' – but then again he was travelling in an Isuzu 4x4.

Only men with harems welcome, obviously. Christine Chambers took this near Kruger National Park.

Clearly no parking for passion wagons – quickies only in front of the Volkswagen factory in Uitenhage, reckons David van der Sandt.

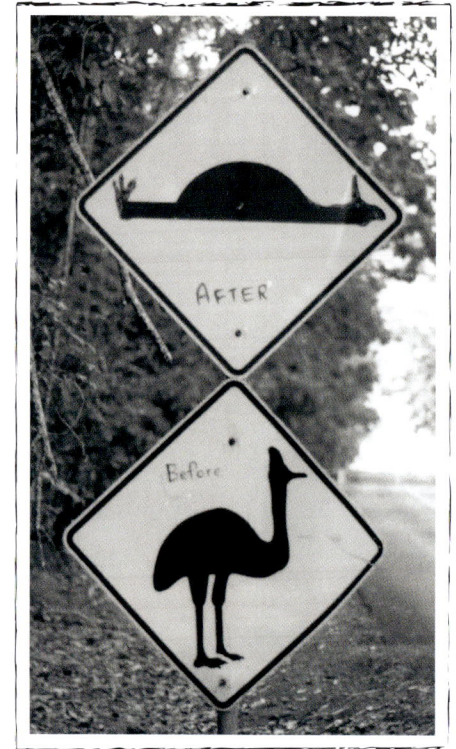

ABOVE: It seems the folks of northern Queensland have found a new way to slow down traffic – cassowary speedbumps. These defaced signs were spotted by Gordon Mayfield of Gordon's Bay between Daintree and Cape Tribulation.

Sometimes the only way to get through to officials is to put it in writing, as P Victor Muller of Stilfontein discovered with this sign in the Northwest Province, between Klerksdorp and Ventersdorp.

If you're not sure what a 'road failer' is just yet, you sure will when your head hits the car roof, as Amalia Legg of Durban discovered as she rode over the damaged road through Swaziland.

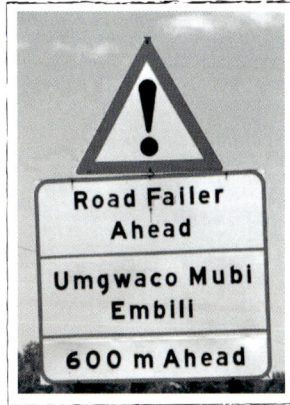

The trees at Khama Rhino Sanctuary in Botswana must be having a tough time trying to grow straight. But isn't this a baobab? Wow! From Ben and Muriel van Rensburg.

Perhaps a little bit of wordplay and a dose of shock factor gets the message across on this sign taken by Grant Pearson on the road between Joburg and Sun City.

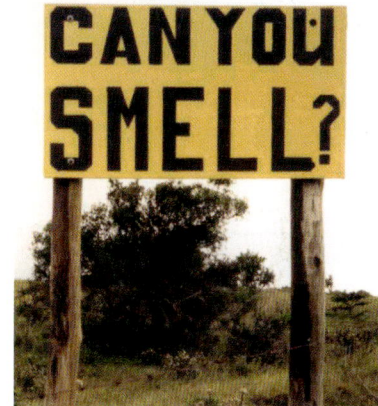

ABOVE: What? The cow dung? Sonja Fourie from Gansbaai, who photographed this sign near East London on the road to Port Alfred, realised it referred to the pastries and coffee up the road at the craft centre. But unfortunately their aroma wasn't strong enough to reach that far.

RIGHT: Sort of like heavy flying fish, perhaps? Do they flap or levitate? This is on Zambia's Great Eastern Highway. Dave Busschau, Nelspruit.

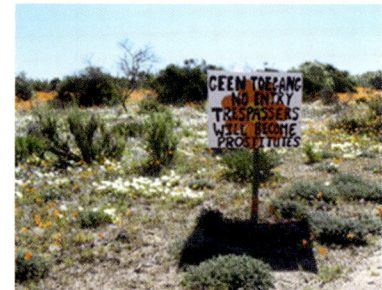

MJ Van Heerden took this photo in Namaqualand. We wonder whether they took to their new role with enthusiasm?

A graffiti artist went to a lot of trouble to tell motorists the truth. From Ian Whittle.

Some signs leave you in no doubt about their message. This is at a boom gate in a yacht club in Spain. From Penny Kayton.

NOTICE

Be careful with personal property

Please tell reception immediately if you lose your sense of humour

They get serious about humour at Ngepi Nature Reserve. Taken by Susan Venter of Tzaneen.

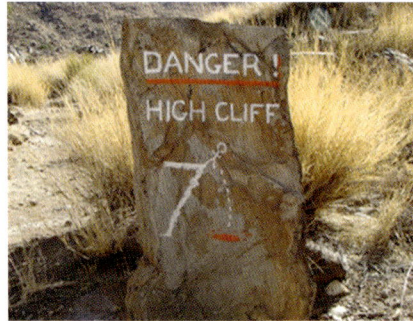

Just in case you can't read. This is at the Weener Gateway to Gamsberg trails. From Rodney Willcox.

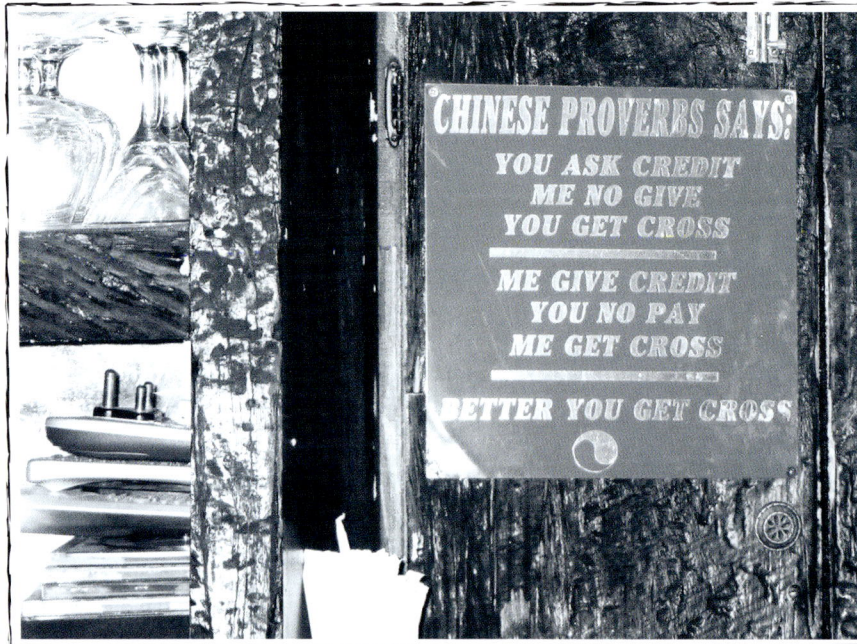

CHINESE PROVERBS SAYS:

YOU ASK CREDIT
ME NO GIVE
YOU GET CROSS

ME GIVE CREDIT
YOU NO PAY
ME GET CROSS

BETTER YOU GET CROSS

This sign is in a pub at Bundu Inn in Mpumalanga. Perhaps the barman was Chinese. Jerry Mamabolo, Limpopo.

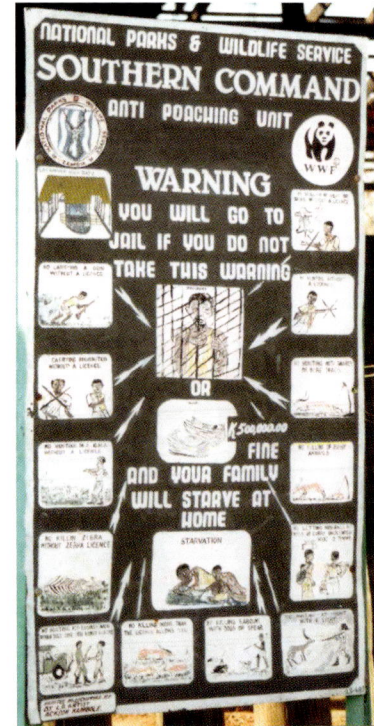

Can't get any clearer than this. Stop poaching or else... Taken in Lochinvar National Park and sent in by Brent Coverdale.

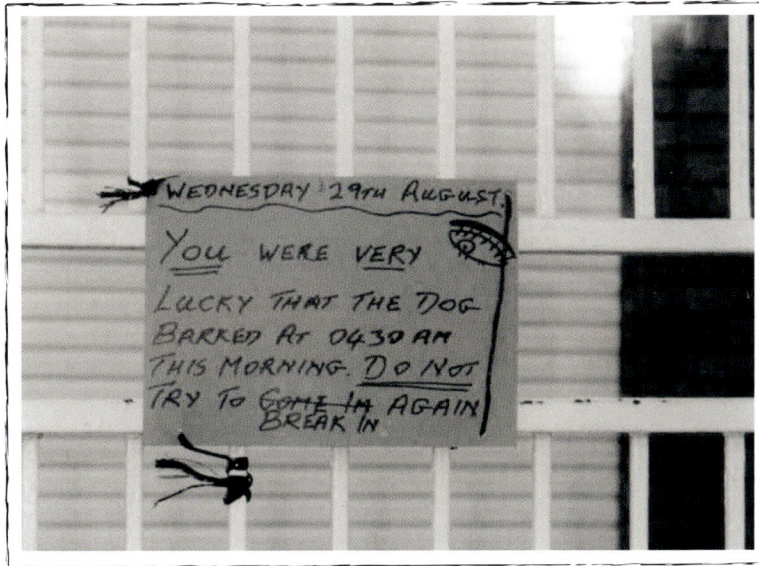

Better the dog gets you before the owner was the warning Sandy Jardine snapped in Gauteng.

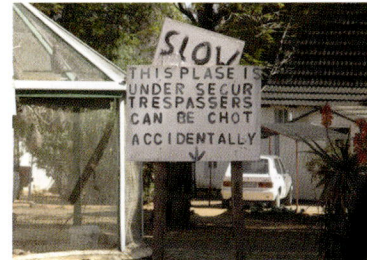

We got out of there quickly, just in case we got 'CHOT ACCIDENTLY'. Brad and Joli, Johannesburg.

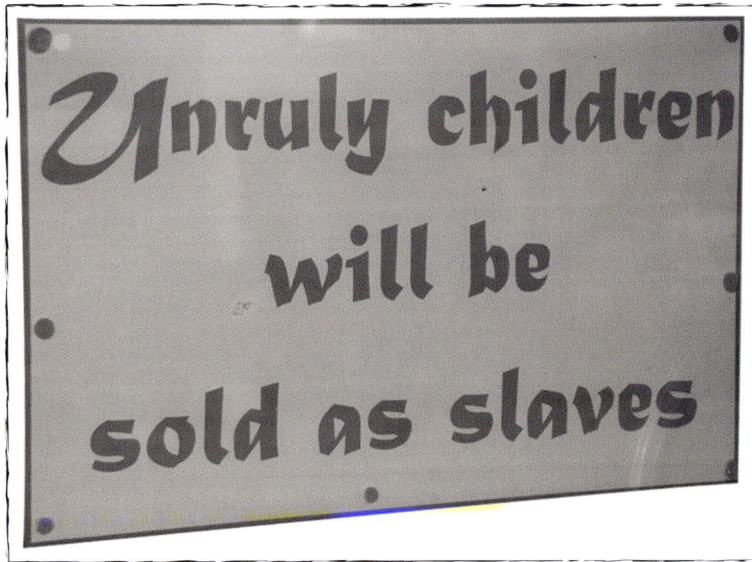

Naughty children beware! David Ritchie, Plettenberg Bay.

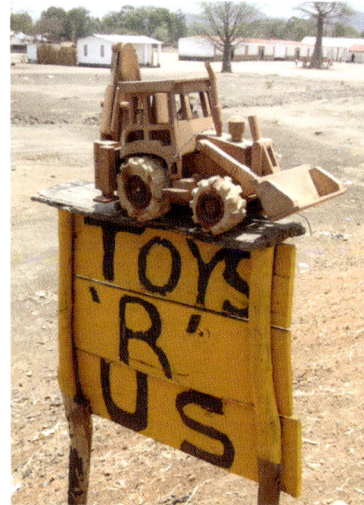

Shopping for kids in Malawi? This 'store' has a maximum exposure position on the road between Monkey Bay and Cape Maclear at the southern end of Lake Malawi. Lucy Bale, Malawi.

I came across this sign in Uganda, close to the Equator and a few kilometres from the River Nile. Brian Wilkins.

This gives new meaning to school transport, says Kevin Tarr. Taken at Mida Creek at Watamu, Kenya.

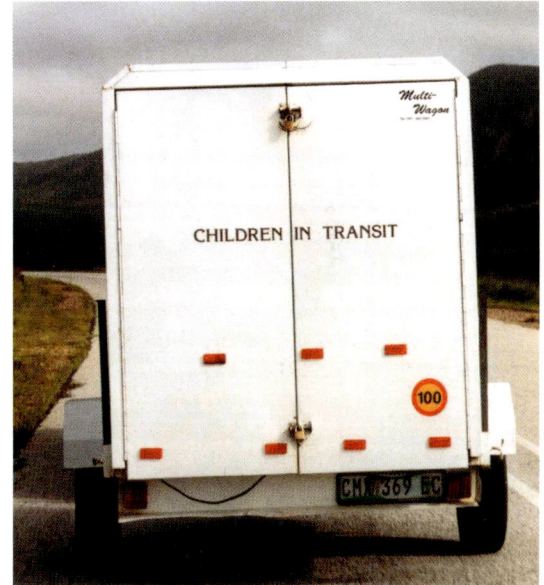

We weren't sure from the photo if there were air holes and fodder troughs in this human horse box. But Sharon Wicks from Port Elizabeth investigated and found the kids, from Woodbridge School in the Eastern Cape, were safely in the vehicle towing it.

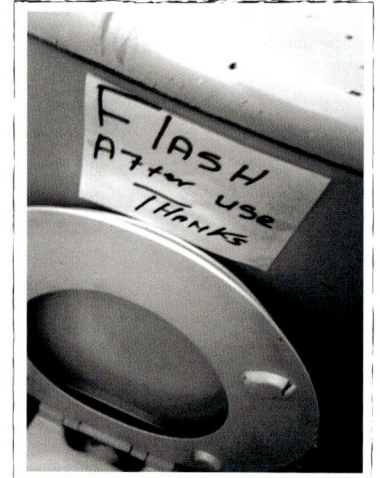

Just make sure you're not sitting down when it happens. Wesley Lazarus found this toilet in Pietermaritzburg.

R Schoombee found herself parked outside a set of upper-class toilets in Mabalingwe Nature Reserve near Bela Bela – a cut above the usual bush experience.

UPPER CLASS TOILETS ⇨ PARKING ⇨

RIGHT: The photo was taken in the Mabalingwe Nature Reserve at the Kalahari Oasis. Danie Malherbe.

BELOW: All 'aboard! Taken by JJF Meyer in Guinjata Bay, Mozambique.

NEW TOILET NO WATER SMELL FLIES FIG TREE ⬅ FOR INSIDE HOUSE OR OUTSIDE

Now that is innovative plumbing! A toilet that doesn't need water? Diane Bannatyre found this charming sign in Limpopo.

OUTBOARD INBOARD

TOILETS

The LOO with a VIEW
The longest 'Long Drop' in Africa!

If it's that deep, we hope the seat holds when you sit on it. Taken at Lake Eland in the Oribi Gorge by Menoli Gounden of Durban.

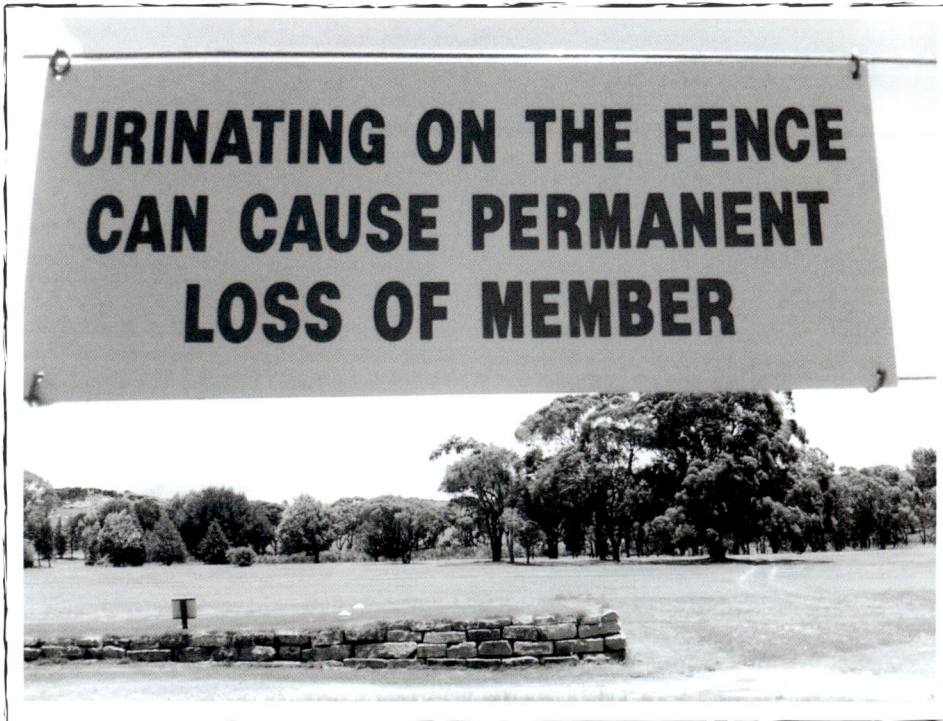

URINATING ON THE FENCE CAN CAUSE PERMANENT LOSS OF MEMBER

This sign at the golf clubhouse in Dordrecht, Eastern Cape, could be deemed shocking news. Charl Strydom.

SPECIAL ATTENTION: LOVELY CUSTOMER

PLEASE FLASH THE TOILET AFTER USE

FROM: PUNDA GATE OFFICIALS

Flush = wash out!

Jo-Anne Stead says that after flashing the toilet at the Mounda Maria gate, in the Kruger National Park, a few times it still didn't wash out.

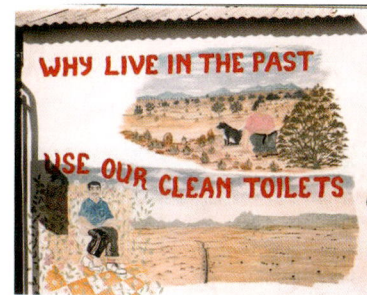

WHY LIVE IN THE PAST

USE OUR CLEAN TOILETS

No more squat, squirt or shake at this 'clean loo' garage in Karasburg, Namibia. Jill Marais of Johannesburg.

All are welcome. Eulala Hards found this sign in Australia.

Brings new meaning to the phrase toilet break. Grahame Mcleod sent us this sign taken in Botswana.

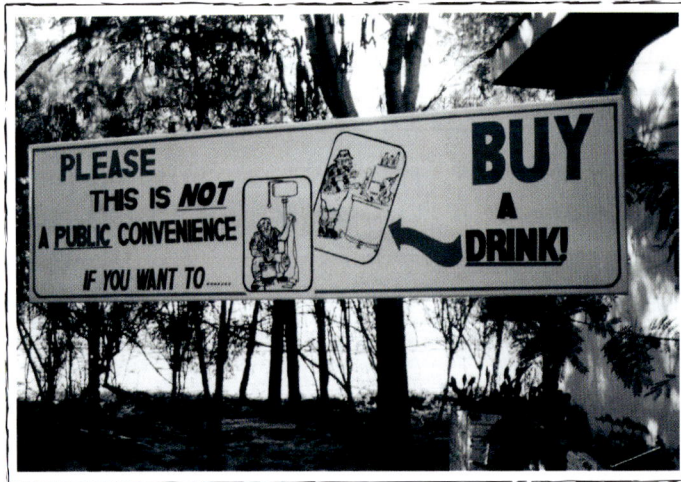

PLEASE
THIS IS *NOT* A PUBLIC CONVENIENCE
IF YOU WANT TO.......

BUY
A
DRINK!

Umm.... Is anyone else confused? The notice is more like an instruction for a Twister game. Selwyn Pogir found it in Linga Linga, Mozambique.

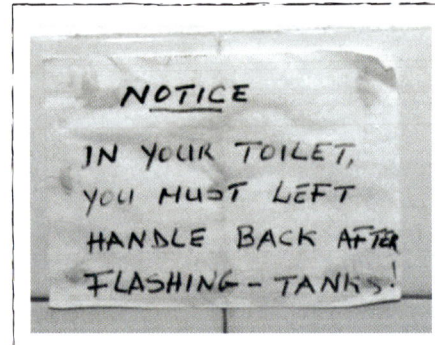

NOTICE

IN YOUR TOILET, YOU MUST LEFT HANDLE BACK AFTER FLASHING - TANKS!

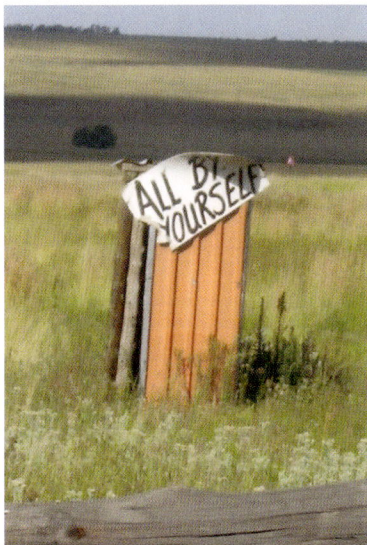

BELOW: Promise no-one is watching. This was taken not too far from a curio shop just before Harrismith by Angi Oliver.

'I know everybody is always in a hurry,' writes Willie Steyn, 'but isn't this pushing it a bit far?' This was in front of a restaurant in Ventersdorp.

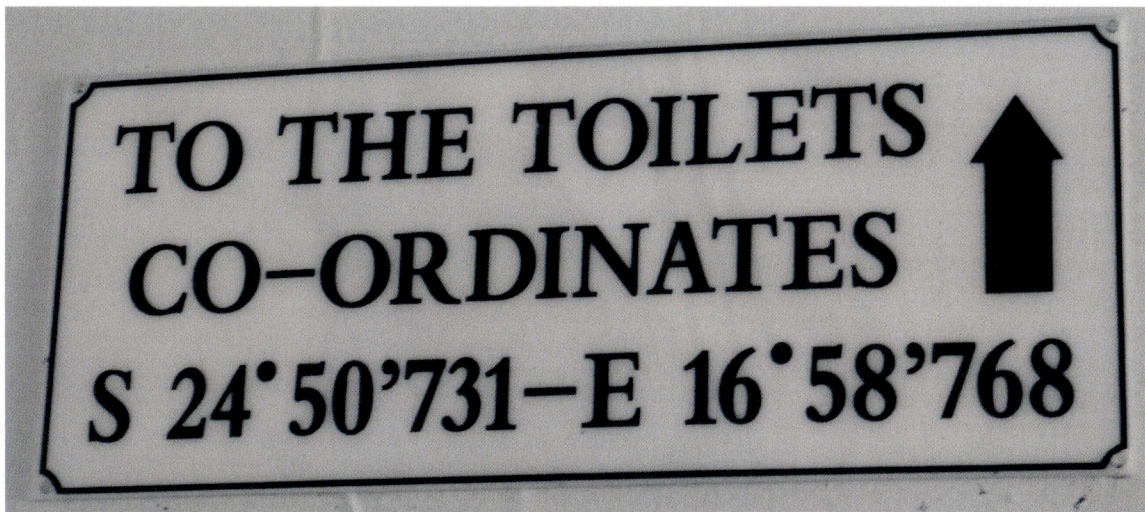

If you're looking for the loo in Maltahohe, Namibia, you clearly need a GPS, says Shaun Gray from Durban.

On whose foot? Or does this wise owl just understand the benefits of walking for exercise? Neila Gunns.

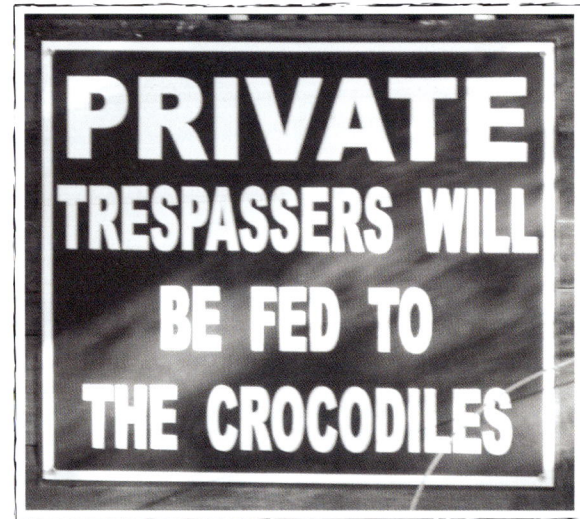

This brings to mind the phrase 'killing two birds with one stone'. From Ildiko Szabo.

We wonder how the plovers and tortoises get out of the potholes? This is on the access road to the lighthouse at Cape St Francis in the Eastern Cape, sent by Bryan Groom.

CROCODILES ARE STRICTLY PROHIBITED FROM MAKING NOISE. WHILE PEOPLE ARE PEACEFULLY SUNBATHING IN THEIR POND AND VICE VERSA. IN HARMONY WITH NATURE.

Earlier in the year on a visit to Kyle Recreational Park near Masvingo, Zimbabwe, we came across the sign requesting the crocs to leave us in peace while sunbathing.

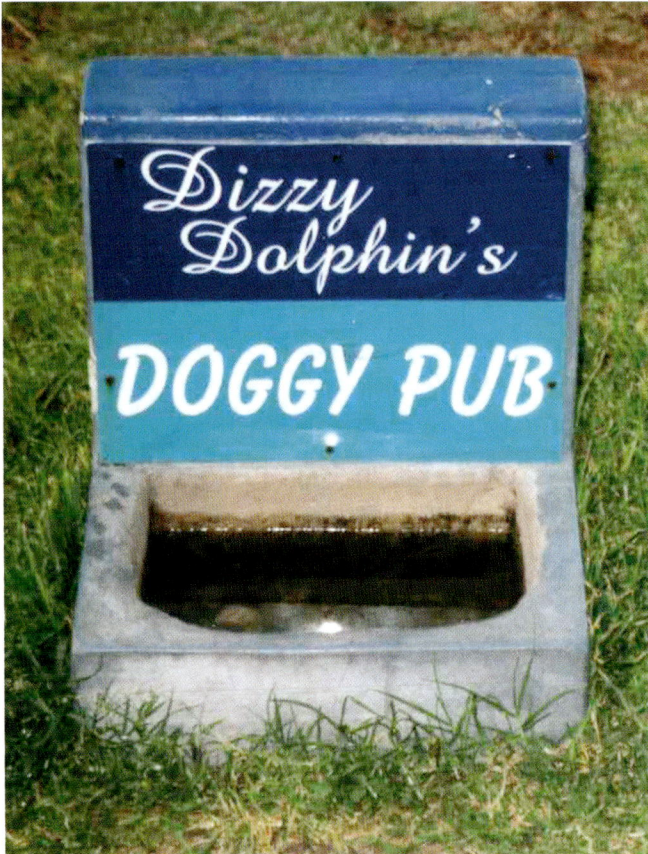

Now that is consideration. Brigette Fouche of Lime Acres found a pub in Port Elizabeth that made man and his best friend feel right at home.

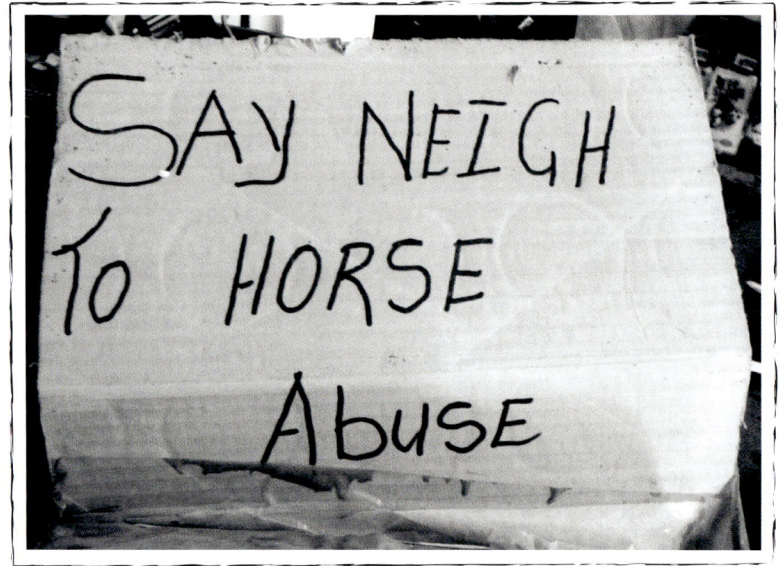

Apparently, Namibia has a big problem with horse abuse. Sent by Menoli Gounden of Durban.

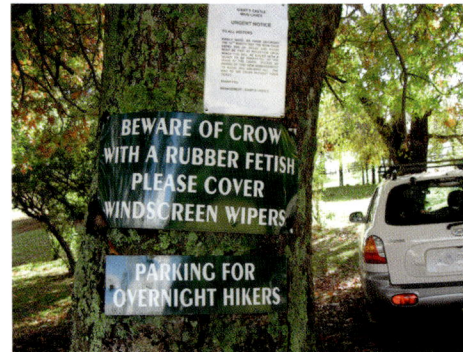

Wonder what else the wildlife gets up to? Malcolm Wilkie, United Kingdom.

You'd be batty to park under this tree at the Pumula Hotel in Umzumbe, KZN. Sent by Mrs Wegerle of George.

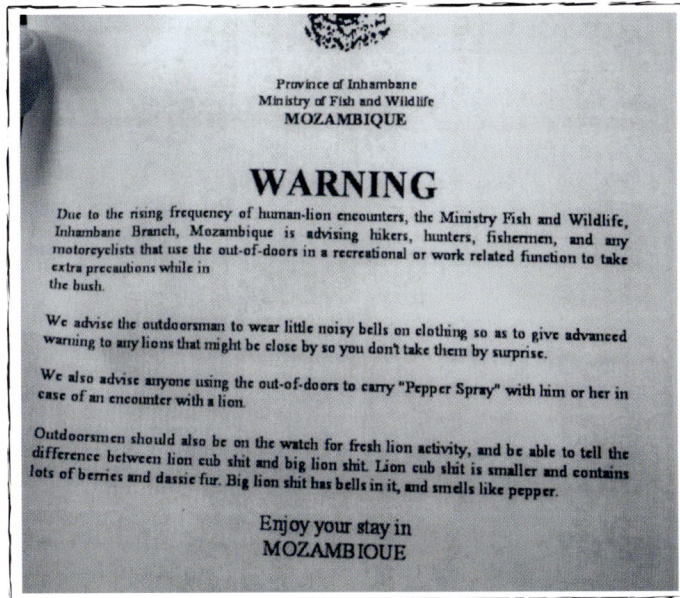

Province of Inhambane
Ministry of Fish and Wildlife
MOZAMBIQUE

WARNING

Due to the rising frequency of human-lion encounters, the Ministry Fish and Wildlife, Inhambane Branch, Mozambique is advising hikers, hunters, fishermen, and any motorcyclists that use the out-of-doors in a recreational or work related function to take extra precautions while in the bush.

We advise the outdoorsman to wear little noisy bells on clothing so as to give advanced warning to any lions that might be close by so you don't take them by surprise.

We also advise anyone using the out-of-doors to carry "Pepper Spray" with him or her in case of an encounter with a lion.

Outdoorsmen should also be on the watch for fresh lion activity, and be able to tell the difference between lion cub shit and big lion shit. Lion cub shit is smaller and contains lots of berries and dassie fur. Big lion shit has bells in it, and smells like pepper.

Enjoy your stay in
MOZAMBIQUE

Okay, okay! We were had. Sent by Ian Bratt of Springs.

There's nothing like good backup for park signage. Taken by Katie Gough in Addo Elephant Park.

Who said animals can't read? From Garth Goosen.

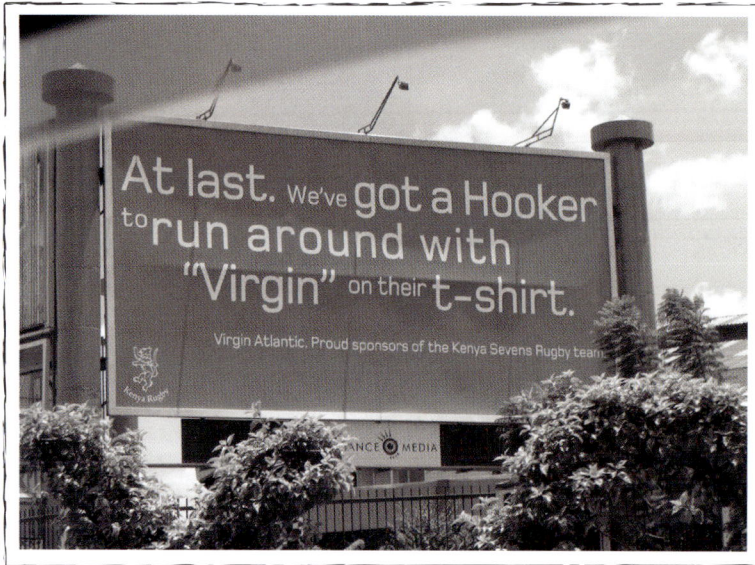

At last. We've got a Hooker to run around with "Virgin" on their t-shirt.

Virgin Atlantic. Proud sponsors of the Kenya Sevens Rugby team

I spotted this in Kenya on the way to Nairobi's airport. Andrew Strachan, Johannesburg.

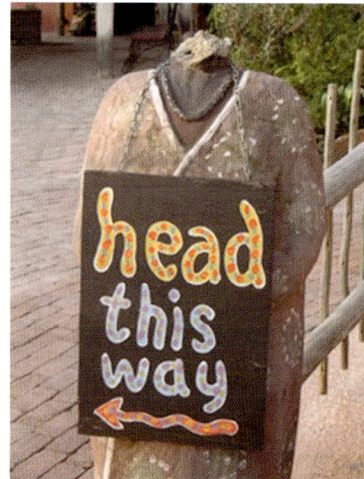

head this way

No need to lose your head. Just keep looking. Sign found in Thokozisa in Central Drakensberg by Vicci du Plessis.

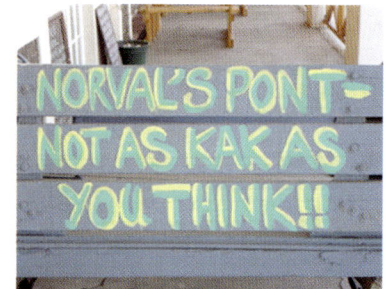

NORVAL'S PONT - NOT AS KAK AS YOU THINK!!

Rob and Meryl Boy took this photo at Norval's Pont Hotel on the way to Bloemfontein via Gariep Dam.

Indeed, it moved very quickly, as Grant Vincent found in the Nuweveld Forest Station near Grabouw.

Phillip van der Merwe sent us this sign from the middle of the Arabian desert.

Now that the grass is brown, do they eat it and jump up and down to make chocolate milkshake? Wes Schoch, KwaZulu-Natal.

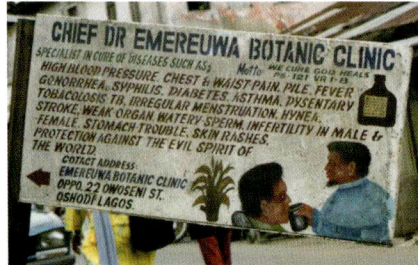

PLEASE NOTE
WE ONLY GIVE
DISCOUNT TO CHARITIES
OR
CUSTOMERS OVER 90
ACCOMPANIED BY THEIR
PARENTS

You'd have to go to extremes to receive a discount at this store. Sent in by VJ Blair.

RIGHT: Is there anything that this healer in Nigeria cannot cure? Sent in by Allan Huntley.

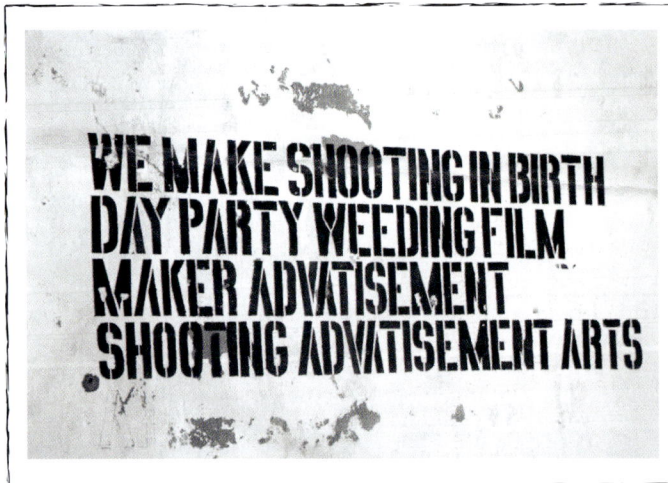

EMERGENCY TELEPHONE

Dial 999 for Coastguard, Police, Fire or Ambulance

Hello operator, I cannot dial emergency. There aren't enough numbers. LBloch says that the phone box is north of London.

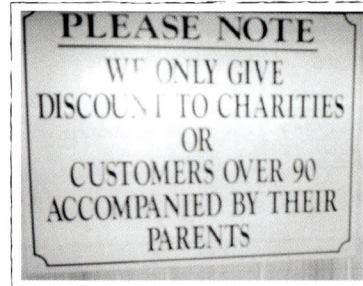

WE MAKE SHOOTING IN BIRTH DAY PARTY WEEDING FILM MAKER ADVATISEMENT SHOOTING ADVATISEMENT ARTS

ABOVE: Let's hope there weren't any casualties in Stone Town. Roger Stringer found this colourfully worded advert by a filmmaker in Zanzibar.

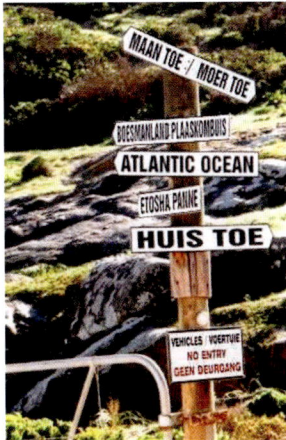

Once you get going on signage, it's sometimes hard to stop. Ulrich Koster snapped this outside the Boesmanland Plaaskombuis on the Cape West Coast.

Catherine Black of Tyger Valley wondered if they were the sort that crept up behind you and brained you with a branch when you least expected it.

Norma Leviton took this photo of 'Eskom specials' at the Austin Roberts Bird Sanctuary in Pretoria.

"ESKOM" Specials
LIGHTS OUT SHOOTER R8
THE GENERATOR Cocktail R17
LOAD SHEDDING Cocktail R20
ENERGY SAVER Cocktail R30

Sorry - No Satellite signal due to permanent "Load Shedding" in this area!

Jammer - Geen Sateliet sein as gevolg van permanente "Beurtkrag" in hierdie deel van die wêreld!

Someone has found humour in the power failures in South Africa. Frank Theron found this sign stuck in a drum in the Kaokoveld, Namibia, so far from anything it just had to be true.

Okay laugh! But in southern Namibia, lawns are as rare as hen's teeth. Karin Swanepoel.

The Zambia Ministry of Education needs to learn to spell what it does. From Lynne Schoeman in Hoedspruit.

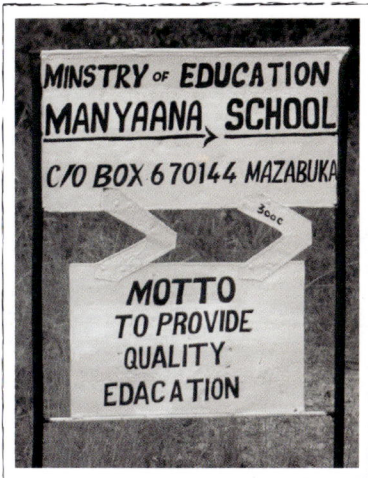

A bright new sign and good wishes is a strong contrast with Ethiopia's wrecked Bahir Dar departure hall in the background, taken by Jurgen Wohlfarter.

Sign? What sign? Vaughn R Swart, Free State.

CAR
WASH

It was fairly quiet until we stopped. Suddenly people emerged from a nearby kraal with water and cloths. Steve Richardson, Kwazulu Natal.

Difference
LIFE
NO GET
DUPLICATE
...DRIVE WITH CARE

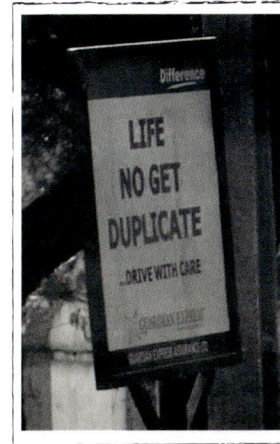

Well, that puts an end to the notion of cloning in Lagos, Nigeria. From Sandy Bing.

MDLALOSE
WE HELP PEOPLE W
HO ARE SHORT
MINDED. P
HO GOT PEOPLE W
NO PARTNERS SEPA
RATE COUPLES
MARRIAGE. PEOPLE
WHO WANT LACK OF MO
NEY IN GAMBLING.

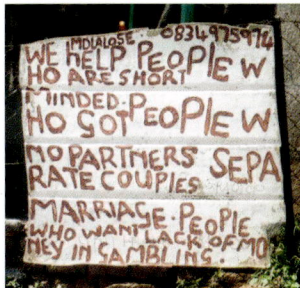

ABOVE: Whether it is the length of your mind or the lack of gambling luck, this traditional doctor in Alexandra township in Gauteng claims to have the cure. Sent by Margaret Can.

ROADSIDE
GEMS
CLEARANCE
SALE

Things can get a little crazy in the summer sale season in Namibia. From Bobby Watson, Cape Town.

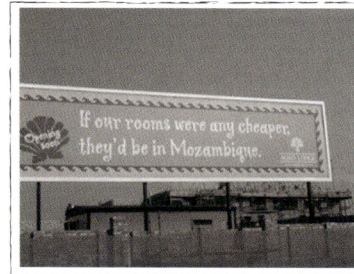

ABOVE: Who says South Africans don't tolerate foreigners? This sign was near the new Road Lodge in Richards Bay. Chris Faure.

ABOVE: Gilly Roberts noticed that they don't lack 'intellectual' reading matter in Njombe.

At the speed this fellow travels, he's very likely to arrive alive, although Adriaan du Toit of Vereeniging, who spotted this near Upington, wondered about the poster of Brad Pitt on the side.

Biggar may not be bigger than New York, but they seem to think it's better.
Mr and Mrs G Jacobs, Free State.

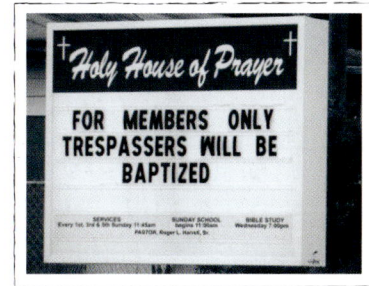

No explanation needed! Taken near Oriental, North Carolina. Mike Meyer.

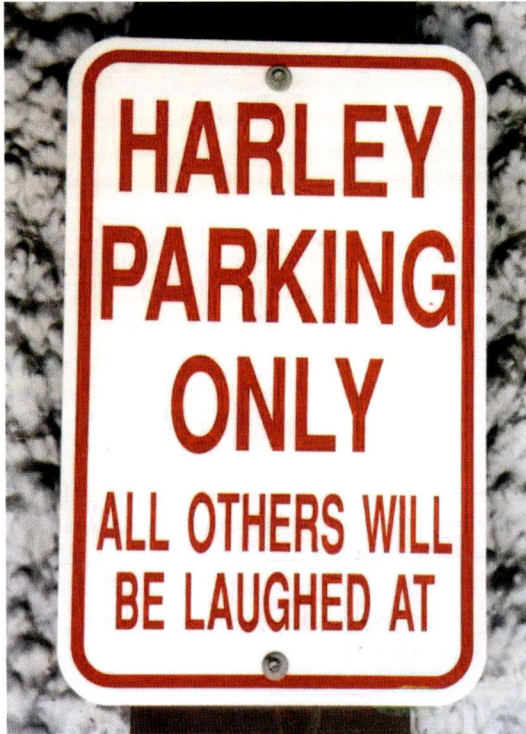

Either you own a Harley or you need a thick skin. Mariza Roussow found this sign in Ashville, USA.

These interesting stats from a summer destination, Seaview Village in New York, must make for lively political debates – in summer. Arthur Jaffe

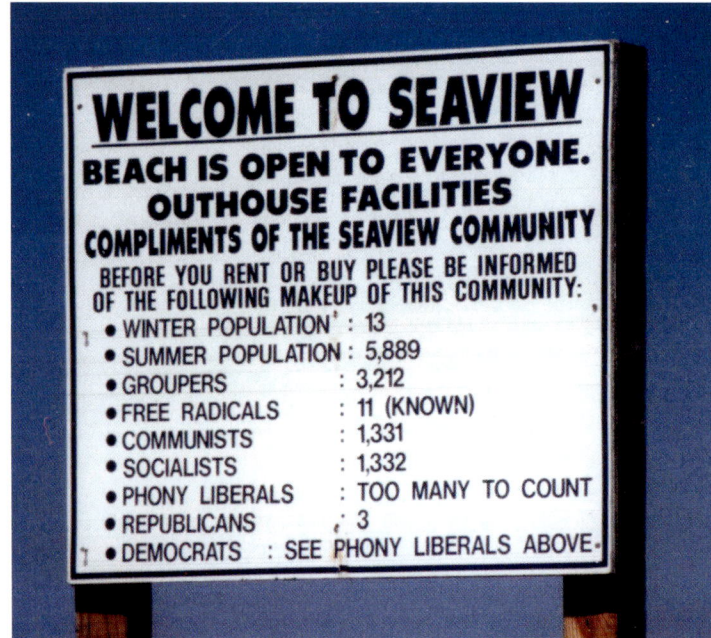

WELCOME TO SEAVIEW
BEACH IS OPEN TO EVERYONE.
OUTHOUSE FACILITIES
COMPLIMENTS OF THE SEAVIEW COMMUNITY
BEFORE YOU RENT OR BUY PLEASE BE INFORMED
OF THE FOLLOWING MAKEUP OF THIS COMMUNITY:
- WINTER POPULATION : 13
- SUMMER POPULATION : 5,889
- GROUPERS : 3,212
- FREE RADICALS : 11 (KNOWN)
- COMMUNISTS : 1,331
- SOCIALISTS : 1,332
- PHONY LIBERALS : TOO MANY TO COUNT
- REPUBLICANS : 3
- DEMOCRATS : SEE PHONY LIBERALS ABOVE

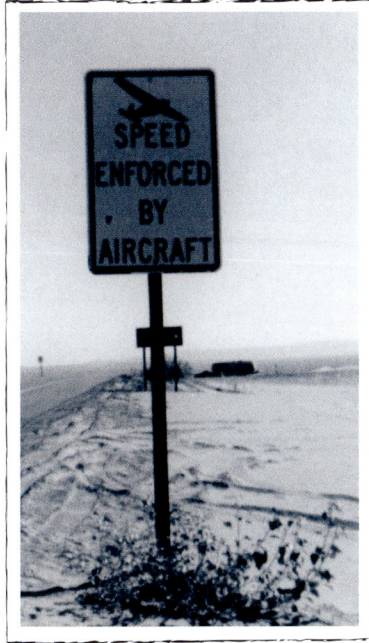

One wonders exactly how the aircraft catch speedsters. Bomb them maybe? Janet Slater took this en route from Las Vagas to San Francisco in the California desert.

These are the sort of signs that can bring about attacks of severe tension if you're given to obeying instructions. Ashlea Brunette took this in California.

ABOVE: Trevor and Zan Gower of Kokstad discovered more than food in a restaurant in Pattaya, Thailand.

ABOVE: Lost in translation, Beijing. Sent by Luke Strugnell.

It's probably safer to stay away from this one stop. Found by Luke Strugnell while on holiday on Beijing.

No, no, no, no, no... is what Beijing Zoo advises when visiting the Giant Panda. Sent by Ohna Norval.

Great, now all smokers can find a fix on the roads. Spotted in Singapore by Joan D'arcy.

POINT
& PISS

SQUAT
& SQUIRT

Look before you sit at the luxury Regal Cinema in Pakistan, suggests Andrew Beadle of Randpark Ridge.

A Zen moment at the Beijing Zoo, experienced by Cynthia and Achim Ecker.

请勿跨越围栏，
以免发生危险！
PLEASE DON'T CROSS ANY RAILINGS
LEST SUDDENNESS HAPPENS！

禁止翻越！
Don't Get Over

Riaad van der Merwe of boksburg saw this sign in China and wasn't sure if people there were in the habit of climbing over very high walls or something more philosophical.

This sign on a tour bus on Lantau Island, Hong Kong, got us giggling. Donna and Frikkie.

NOTICE

IT IS AN OFFENCE IN LAW FOR

PASSENGER TO TALK TO A DRIVER.

残疾人厕位
DEFORMED MAN LAVATORY

Michelle Sacks found this Chinese translation a little tactless.

本餐厅谢绝自带酒水
The restaurant declined its own wine

My daugter sent me this by e-mail. Liz Smith.

请勿乱扔杂物
PLEASE DON'T THROW RUBBISH AWAY
ごみを拾てないでください

Riaad van der Merwe ended up with a lot of trash in his pockets after reading this sign in China.

DOOR SPOILT
门坏

We wonder if they caught the person who spoiled it? Shane Hona found this sign in Singapore.

BELOW: It seems that in Ireland, after a couple of Guinesses, they can walk through walls. Keith Davidson, Jeffreys Bay.

BELOW: Maybe they weren't doing so well after all. Estelle McDonald Paterson found this sign in England.

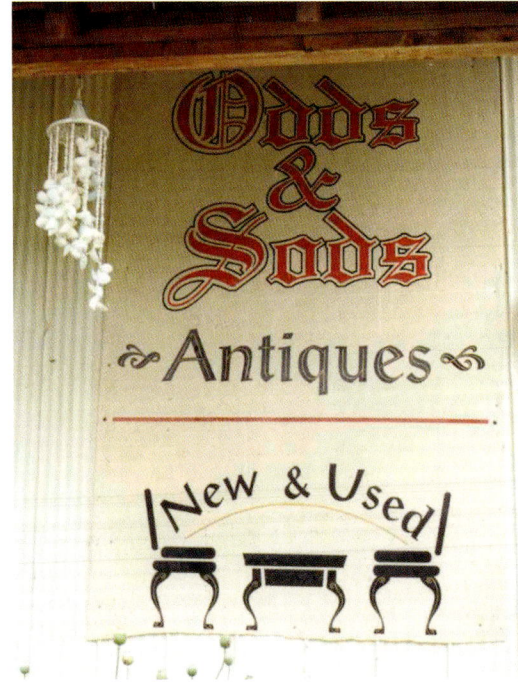

I wondered what a new antique looked like? But this shop in Canada seemed to have an idea. Jerry Waasdyk, Kempton Park.

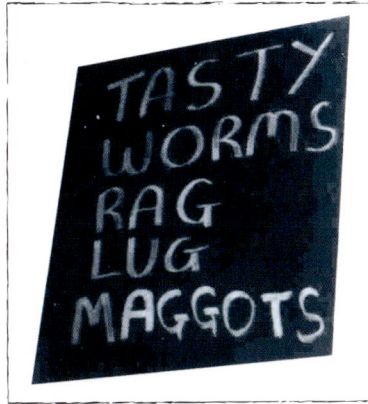

RIGHT: Maggot soup, yum! Pip and Beryl Fuller of Highlands North thought twice about eating at this fishing shop turned restaurant in Cornwall, England.

Pelicans in London be worried – if you don't want to be humped, try flying across instead. Garin Denysschen, Hillcrest.

This very inviting bench was below the old priory, at the end of Tynemouth pier in Newcastle, England. Mark Stier, United Kingdom.

Obviously www.arachnid.com! This was spotted in Bourton-on-the-Water by Ken Nurden of Pretoria.

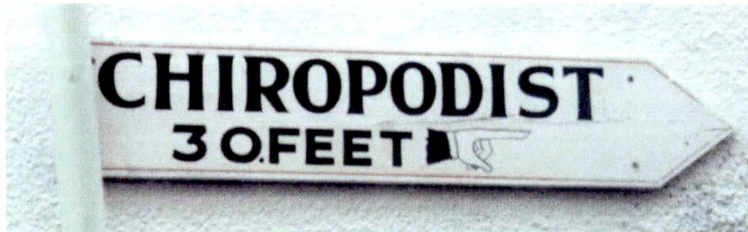

BELOW: They shouldn't wonder if any South Africans walk straight past them. Juanita Reichgelt sent this sign taken in Walthamstow, London.

BELOW: If you're a chiropodist with a sense of humour, a sign like this is irresistible. Taken in Newquay, England, by Pat and David Witten.

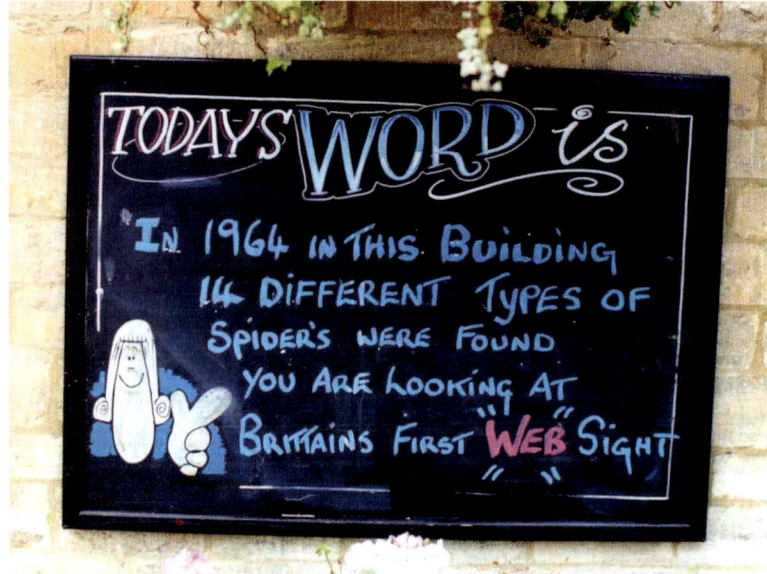

No! Really? Taken in Poole, England, by Brenda Cheverton.

THE
1 HOUR
CRUISE
AROUND
THE
ISLANDS
LASTS FOR
60 MINS.

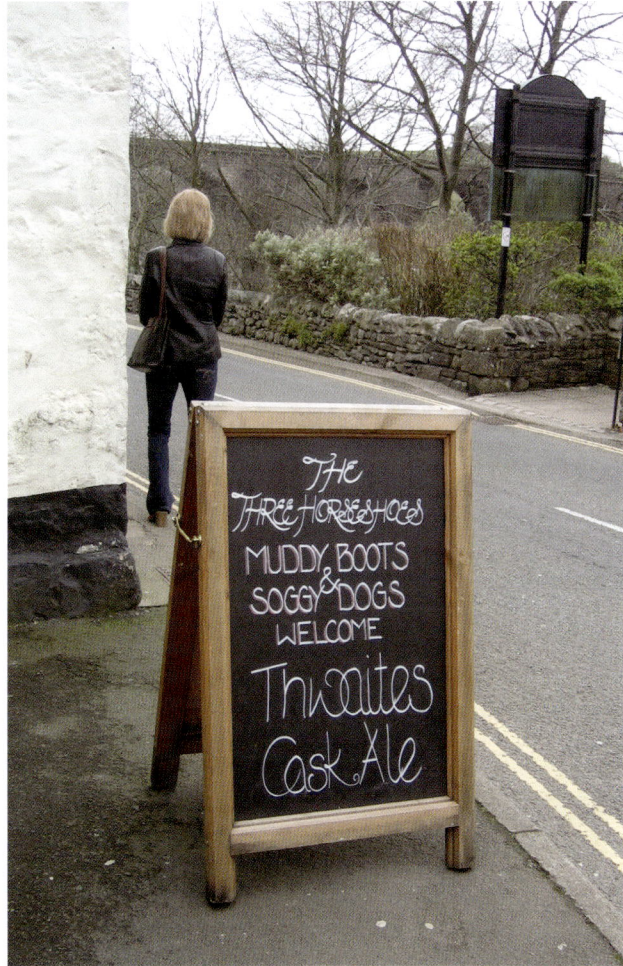

THE
THREE HORSESHOES
MUDDY BOOTS
&
SOGGY DOGS
WELCOME
Thwaites
Cask Ale

In England they're soggy about their pets. Found in Yorkshire by Eleanor Ives.

Christine James found this sign outside a car park in Calais, France. She expected to see thieves wearing berets hiding behind each car!

Taken in Spain on a wall outside the huge Granada Cathedral. Vaughan Paterson of Shrewsbury, England.

Explains the zero population in this part of town, Windsor, Australia.
Sent in by A Pringle.

Found in the car park to the Chinese Restaurant in Te Anau,
South Island, New Zealand. Alan Brooks, Krugersdorp.

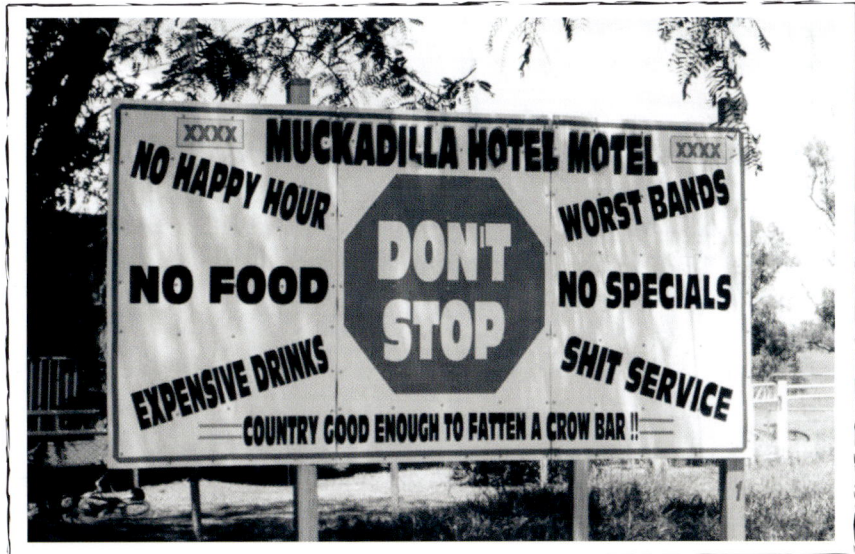

On second thoughts, I'll pass. Gail Daves and John Thompson found this sign outside the Muckadilla Pub in Australia.

Please DO NOT FEED OR TALK TO The MECHANIC!

ALL ENQUIRIES... IN SHOP

The mechanic had probably lost his nuts. Spotted in Australia by Beth Lorden, Kroonstad.

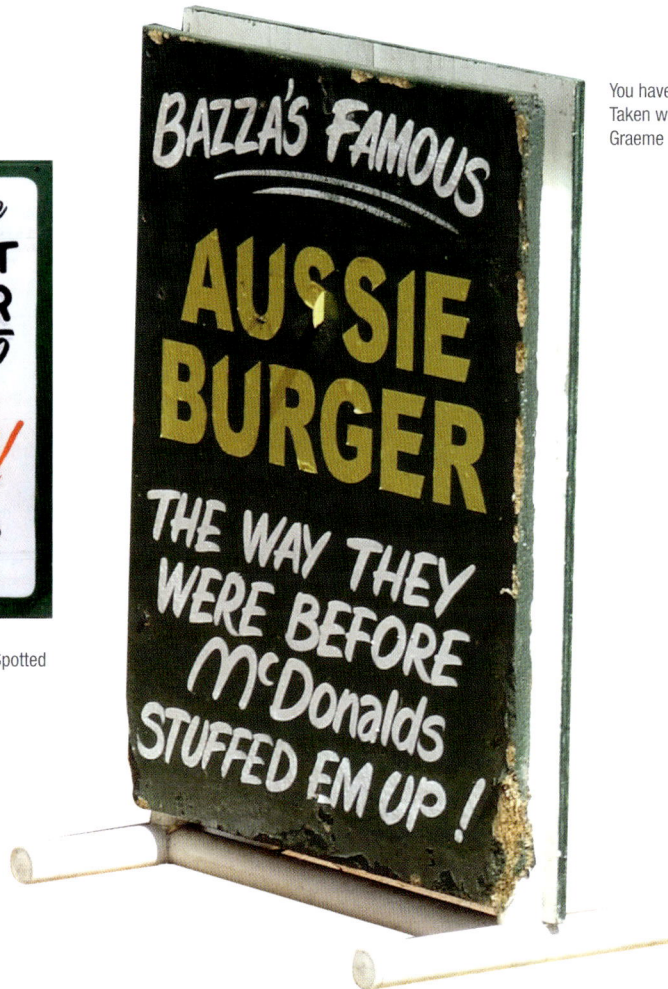

BAZZA'S FAMOUS AUSSIE BURGER THE WAY THEY WERE BEFORE McDonalds STUFFED EM UP!

You have to love their outright honesty. Taken while on holiday in Australia by Graeme Cox, Krugersdorp.

Quick Fokker.

We do Kalgoorlie - Perth in 80 minutes. ▲ SKYWEST

Anyone for a quickie? Only A$45 dollars from Kalgoorlie to Perth. Taken by Sandy Fiulayson, Australia.

In a town called Yass in Australia, Noelette Pearson found this sign and wondered if they knew what they were doing.

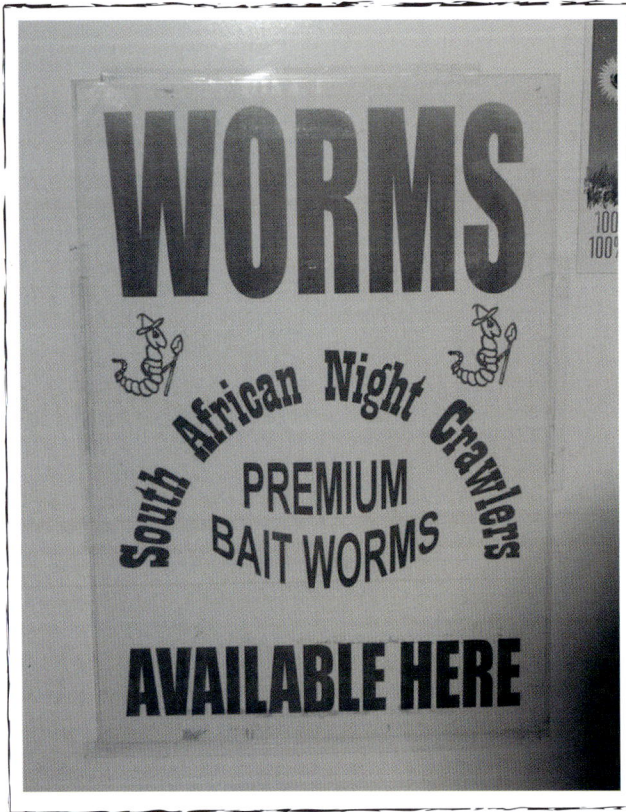

It must take a long time for these worms to get to Murray River in Australia, where this photo was taken, especially as they only travel at night. Snapped by Mark Hardy.

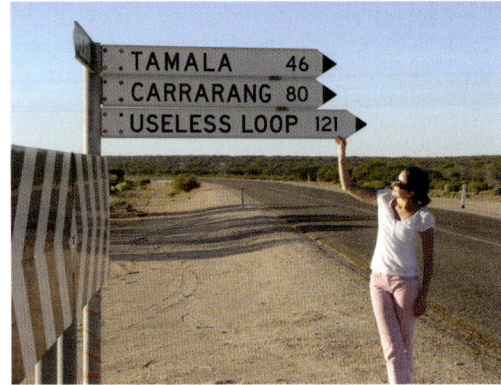

No doubt all the other ways are useful loops. Andre and Marelise van Deventer found this sign in Australia.

While on holiday in Cyprus, Bob Green was sorely tempted to disregard this sign.

ΑΠΑΓΟΡΕΥΕΤΑΙ ΤΟ ΟΔΗΓΗΜΑ
ΕΝΤΟΣ ΤΗΣ ΛΙΜΝΗΣ

DRIVING IN THE LAKE
IS FORBIDDEN

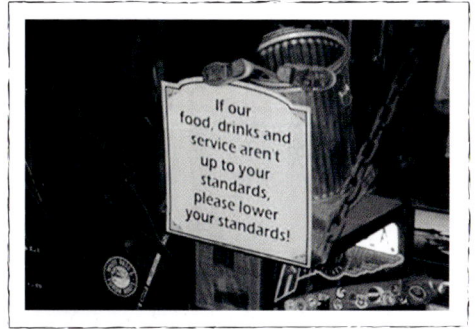

If our food, drinks and service aren't up to your standards, please lower your standards!

The photo was taken in the Red Dog Saloon in Juneau. The saloon is in the original Wild West fashion and a favorite stop in town for a glass of Alaskan Amber. From Johan Wessels.

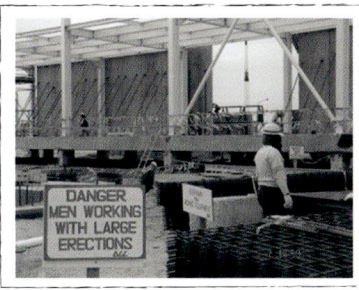

DANGER
MEN WORKING
WITH LARGE
ERECTIONS

Ryan Glenny snapped this sign when he was working in Saudi Arabia and wondered if he'd ever crack the work team.

We wonder if they serve side dishes with their soups on the Greek Island of Samos? Snapped by Gordon Brooker of Pietermaritzburg.

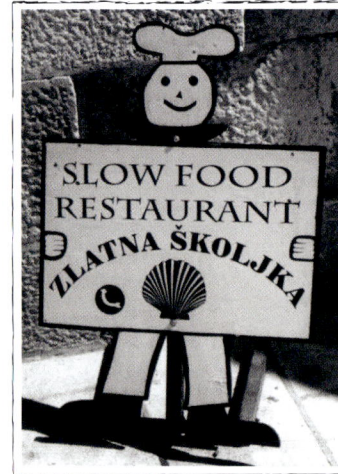

ABOVE: Sick of fast food? Try the Slow Food Restaurant in Croatia. Sent in by Charl and Marietjie Gonin.

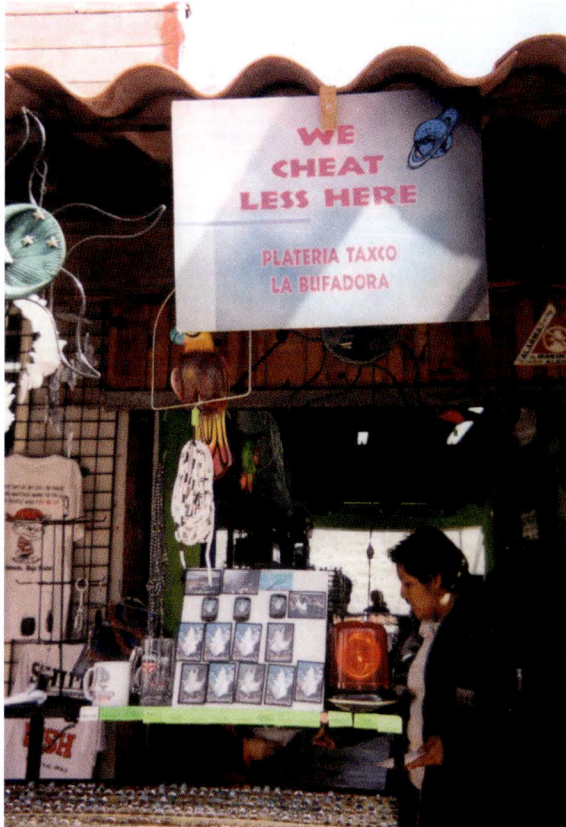

They didn't say that they didn't do it. Found by Alison Morton.

Some countries take all sorts of precautions against lawsuits but this is crazy – the place is a desert. Spotted in Hatta, United Arab Emirates, by Theodora Raubenheimer.

This sign was found in Dubai warning motorists to watch for anything that may jump out of the road and shout 'Surprise!' Hazel Hardie.

BELOW: I wonder if they were really sorry? Istanbul, Turkey. Sent in by Rizwana Osman.

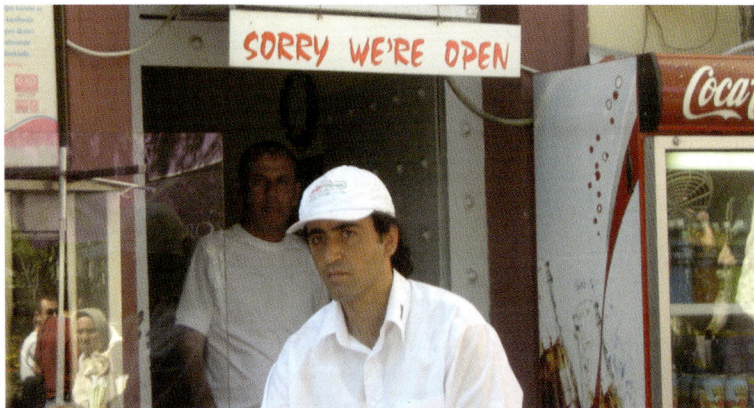

LEFT: As it says, nothing happened on that spot. Sue van Niekerk (Durban) found the most exciting place in Mauritius.

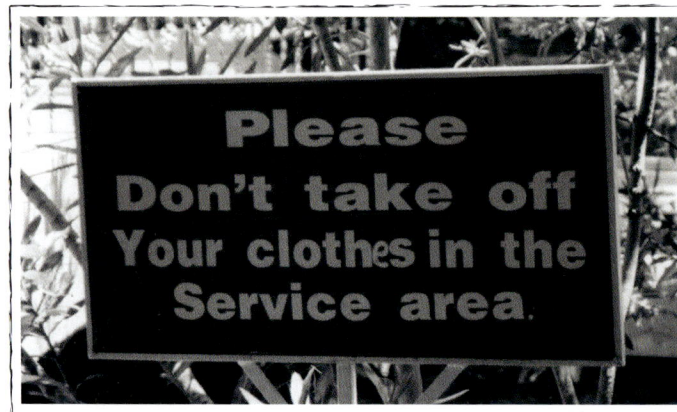

ON THIS SPOT IN 1764 NOTHING HAPPENED!

RIGHT: Brazil is known for speeding banisters – beware! Janet and Lain MacFarlane, Cape Town.

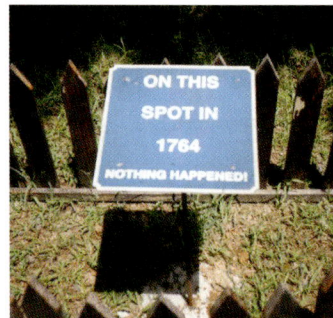

NÃO ULTRAPASSE O GUARDA-CORPO

DON'T OVERTAKE THE BANISTERS

Please Don't take off Your clothes in the Service area.

ABOVE: In Pumukkale, Turkey they prefer you to keep your clothes on until you've been served. Meryl and Derek Russell.

Somewhere in Asia, there are lots of men with black eyes. Seen by Bernard Joemat.

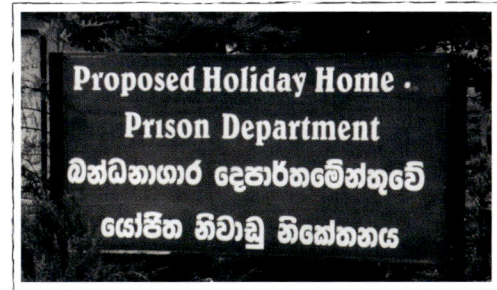

There are clearly prime holiday detention facilities in Sri Lanka. Reto Muller, Switzerland.

I'd also be a little 'nervous' going into surgery here! This was taken in southern Afghanistan by Paul Smith.

The Croatian copywriters at the Cappy ad agency weren't having a good day. This was snapped by Charl and Marietjie Gonin.